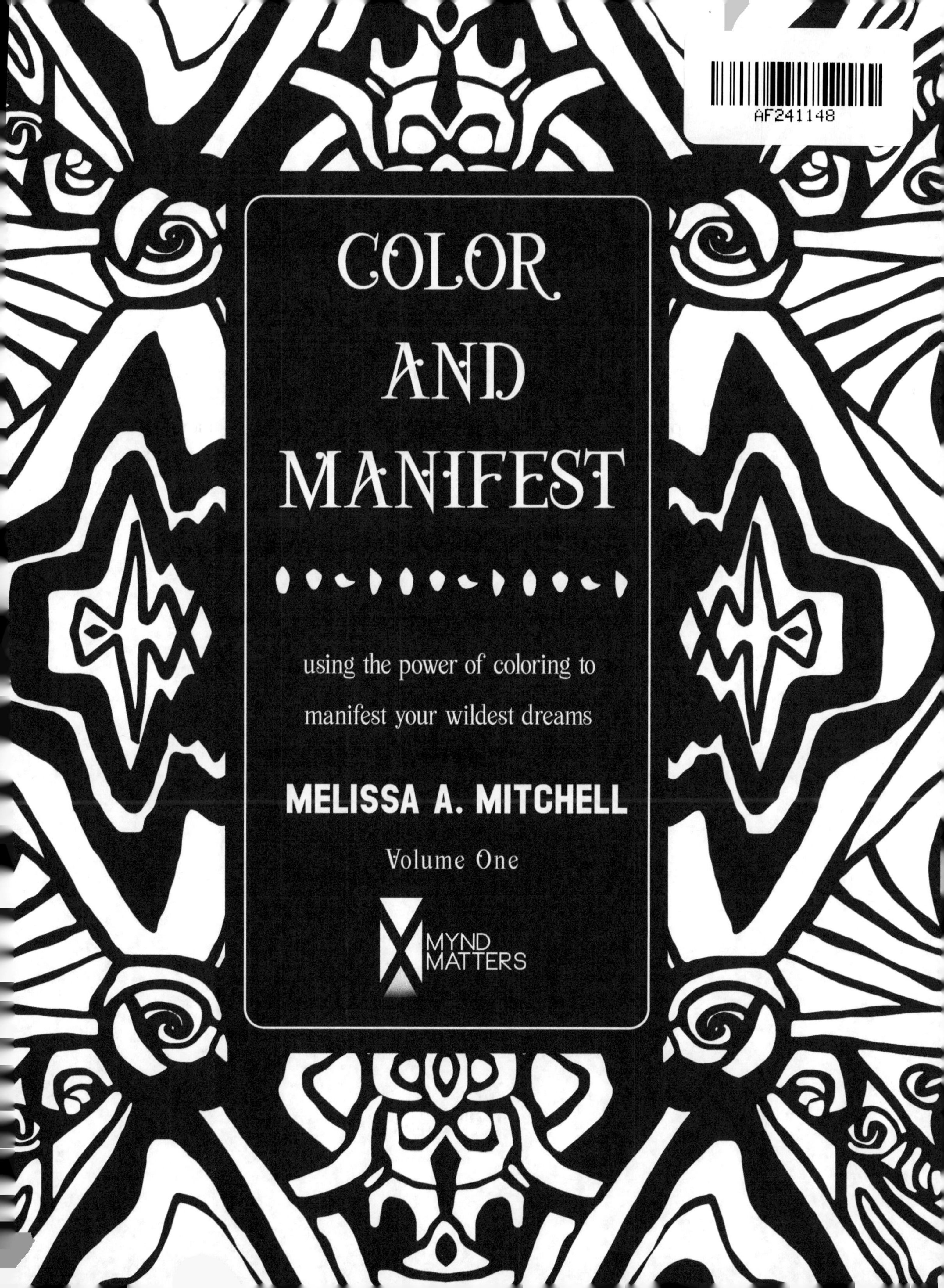

COLOR AND MANIFEST

using the power of coloring to

manifest your wildest dreams

MELISSA A. MITCHELL

Volume One

MYND MATTERS

Mynd Matters Publishing
715 Peachtree Street NE
Suites 100 & 200
Atlanta, GA 30308
www.myndmatterspublishing.com
SBN: 978-1-948145-92-3

FIRST EDITION

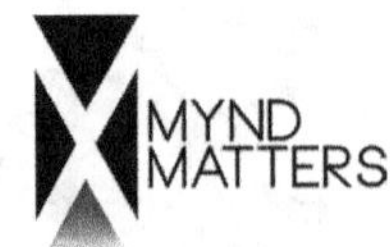

INTRODUCTION

Welcome to the world where you are able to **Color and Manifest** your wildest dreams!

When dreaming up this body of work, I was intentional of when, where, and how I pulled it all together. My goal is to create a space that activates both the left and right sides of your brain and helps propel you towards the power and urgency of this moment. Right now, you have the ability to pick up your tools and change the entire course of your existence. But first, you have to believe it is possible.

When people ask for my "secret formula" or want to know the "best" tips to manifesting, I always chuckle. The answer is YOU. *You are the formula. You are the magic. You are the secret ingredient.* It's been you the entire time.

Imagine finally facing God at the end of your time here on Earth. As God speaks to you, you see and feel colors you have never seen, magically emanating all around you. While standing in awe and amazement, you ask what the colors are and God simply says, "Those are all the blessings you never had the courage to ask or believe for." Let that sink in for a moment. There are things in your life that ONLY have your name assigned to them. No one else qualifies for those blessings but you. It would be a tragedy to live your entire life timid in your beliefs and cowardly in your faith. You deserve ALL that your hearts desires, but it is first going to take some work.

I created **Color and Manifest** in the midst of my own journey. As I am further defining my "who" and "why," I wanted to pull together something memorable. Something I can hold in my hands and always have as evidence of what God was capable of pulling out of me, even when I didn't see the whole way. Like most of the world, I am finding a balance between doing nothing and everything as we endure the impact of a global pandemic. Creating nothing during this season was not an option and historically speaking, some of the greatest literary works and witty inventions were created when "budding" visionaries were isolated to their homes and safe spaces. For 2020, I want to be counted in that number. When my great, great grandchildren are told stories about me, they will have proof through my art, books, wearable art, and my many photoshoots. Won't that be magical?

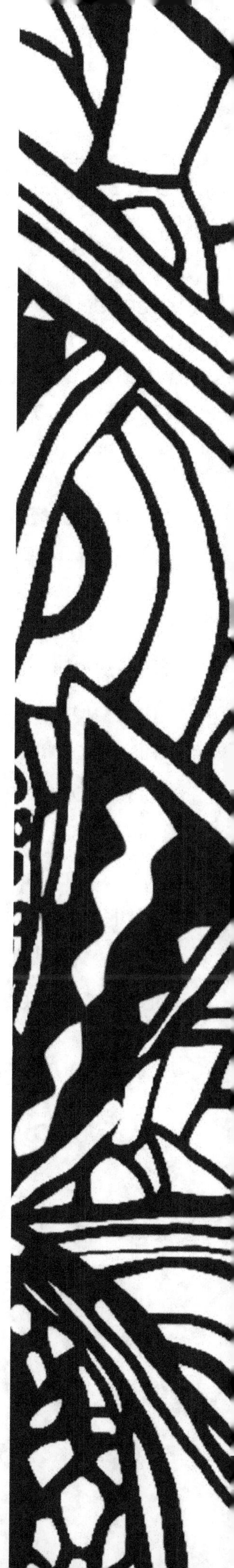

Greatness is born during times like these. Through **Color and Manifest**, allow me to serve as the midwife to your next level. Let me help you cultivate the seeds that have been buried for far too long. It is time to harness the power that you inherently possess. The only rule to this journey is that you wake up every day in golden worthiness. You deserve to see your visions and dreams come into fruition in this lifetime. By picking up some coloring tools (paint, watercolors, crayons, markers, pens, etc.), you will begin to activate parts of your subconscious that needed a little push. This is the sign you have been waiting for. The time is now to be exactly who you dreamed of becoming.

Color and Manifest will help you chronicle what you were birthing while the world was healing and humans were cleaving to one another in quarantine life.

This is your time to focus on your **alignment.**

This is your time to **believe** in yourself.

This is your time to be **consistent**.

This is your time to garner the things you **deserve**.

This is your time to embrace being an **exception** to every rule.

This is your time to remain **grateful** in all things.

This is your time to **visualize** living your best life.

This is your time to understand that you can **manifest** all our deepest dreams and desires.

This is your time.

I pray you **Color and Manifest** yourself right into what God has promised for you.

It is time.

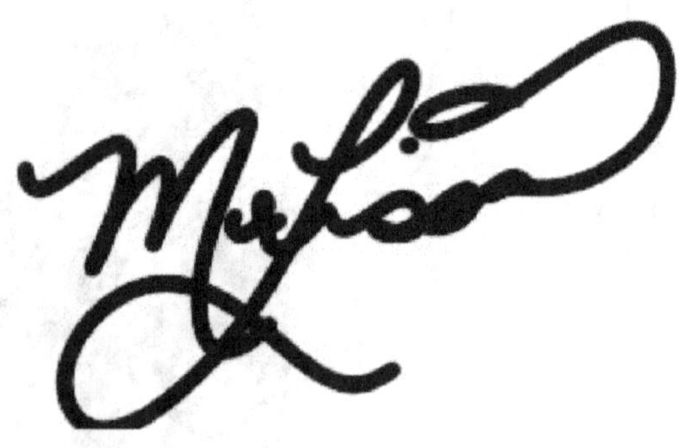

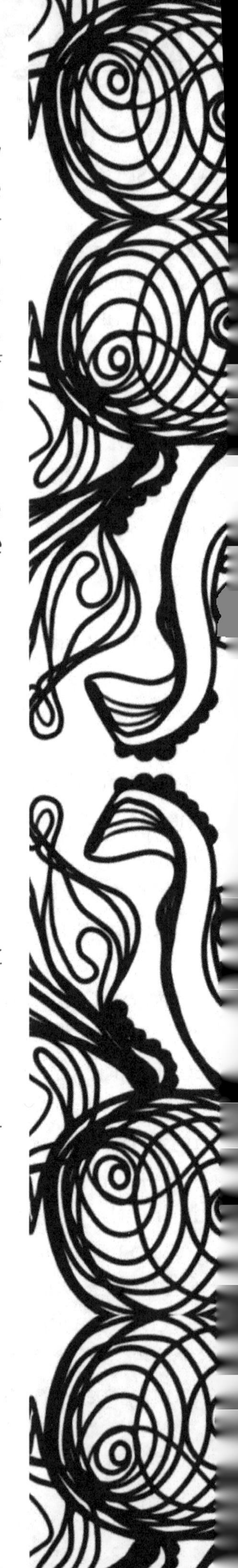

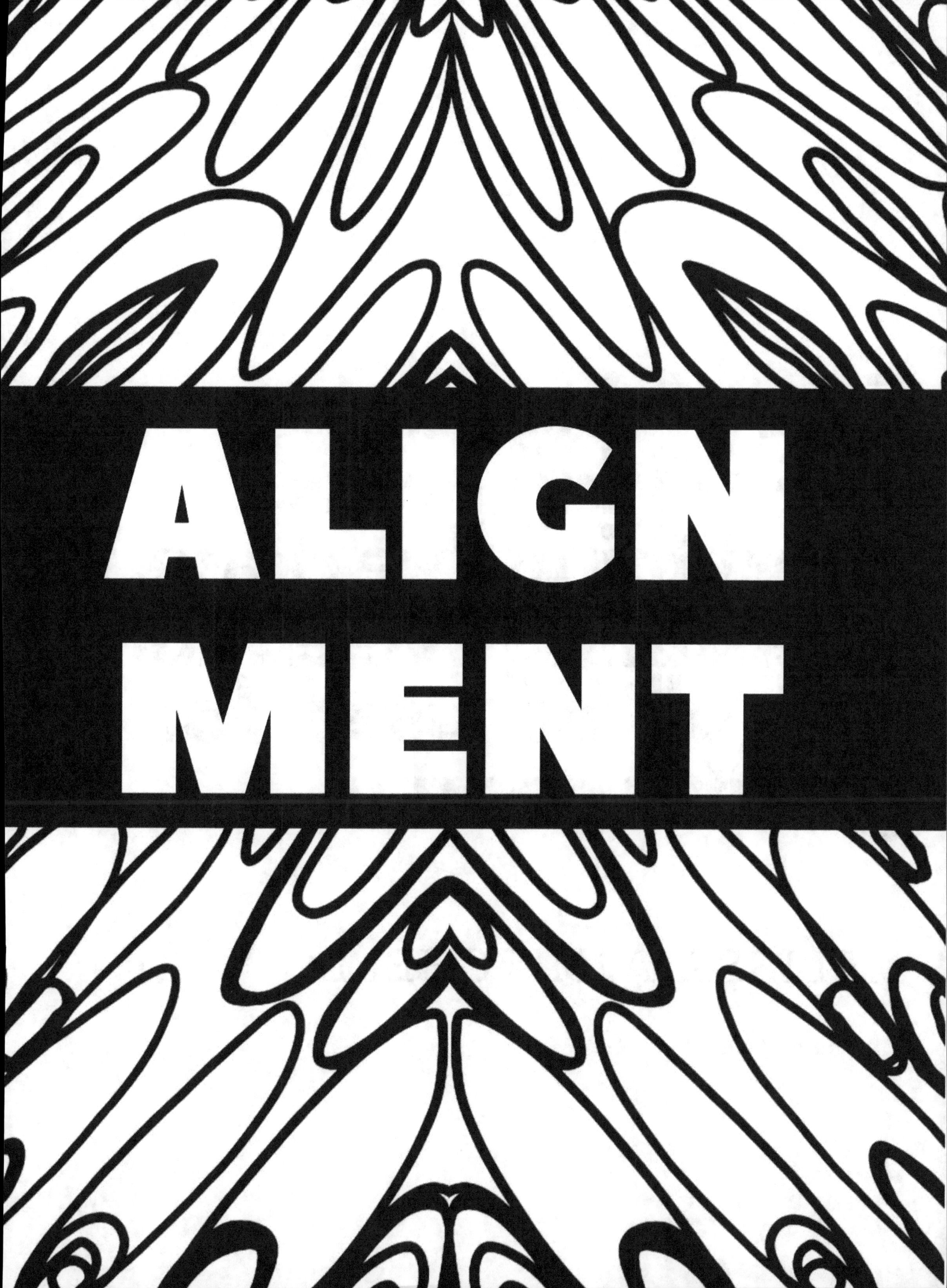
ALIGN
MENT

Everything I am, everything I was, everything I've done, & everything I've endured, will all be used for my greater good.

MELISSA A. MITCHELL

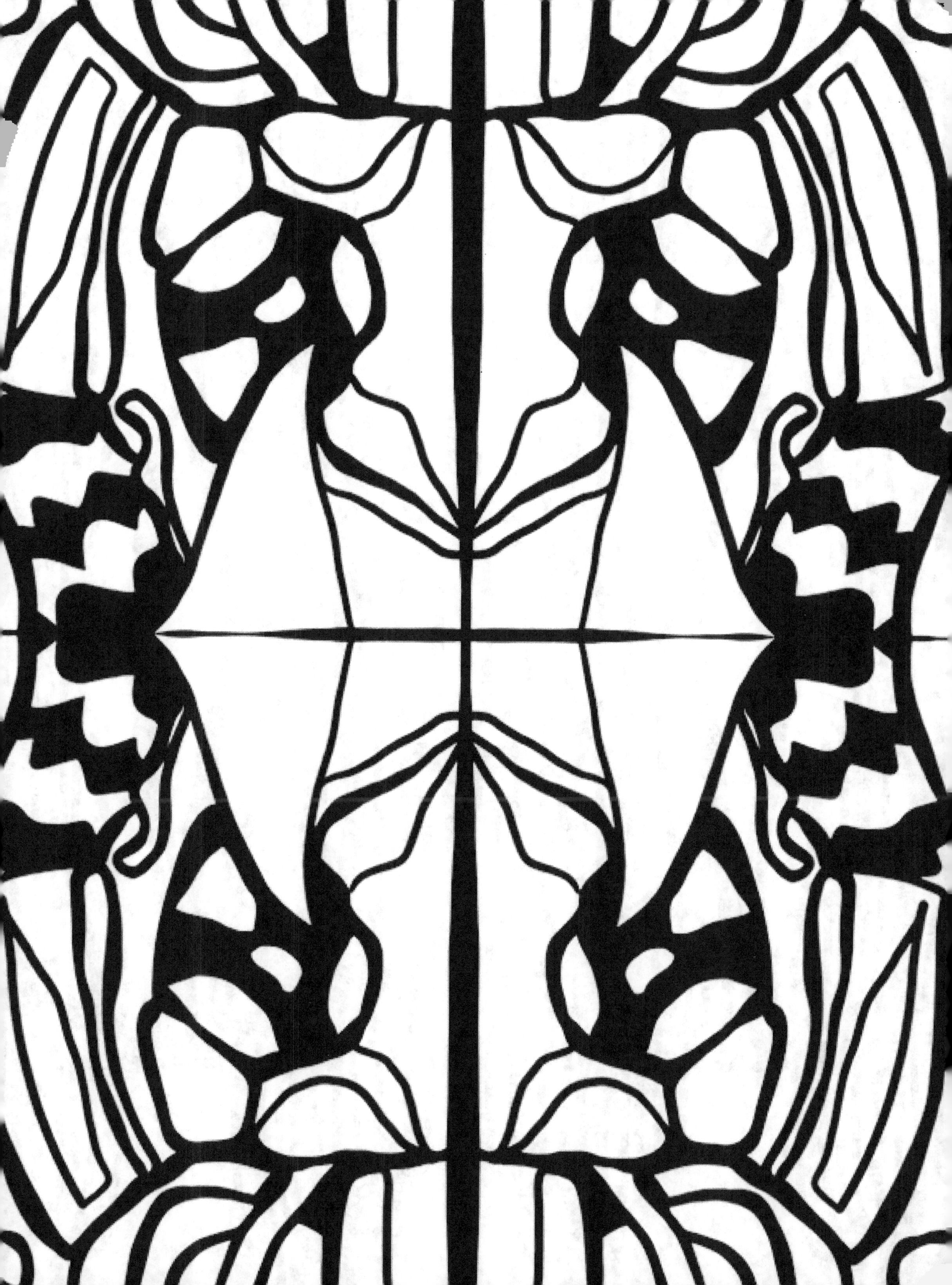

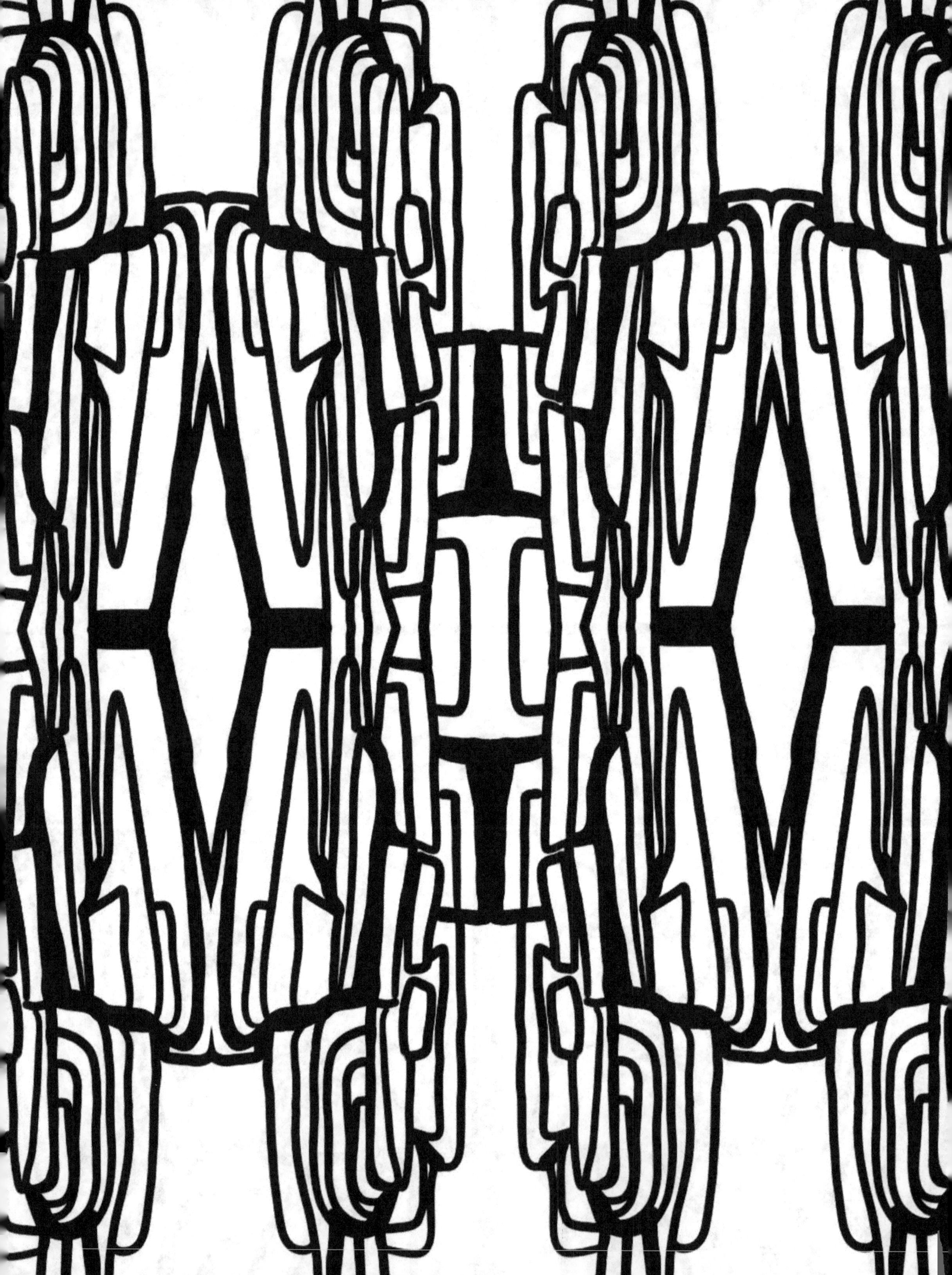

What needs to happen now, for me to be where I need to be?

Date & Time _______________

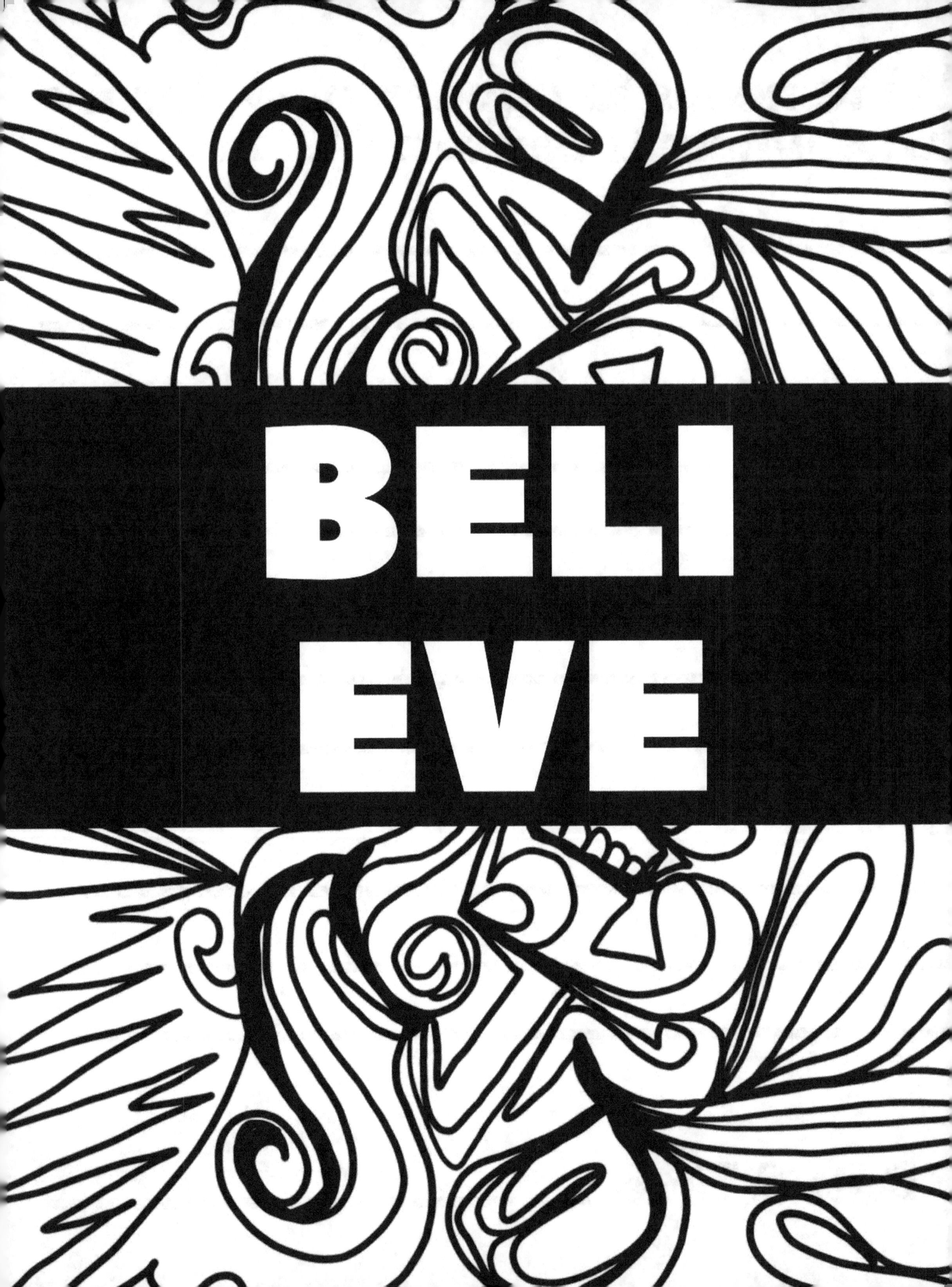
BELI
EVE

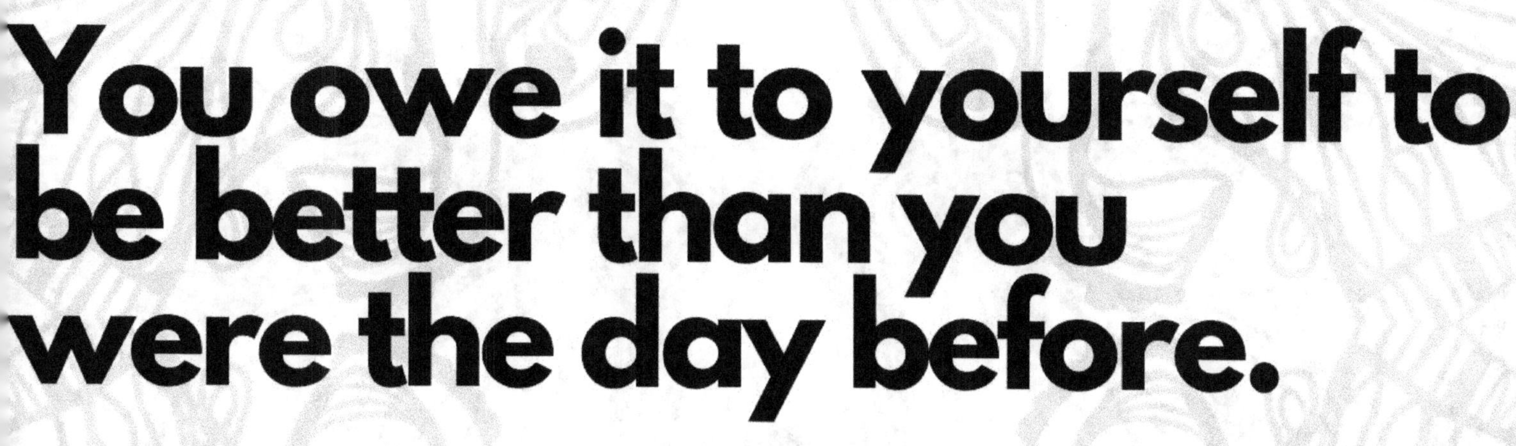

You owe it to yourself to be better than you were the day before.

MELISSA A. MITCHELL

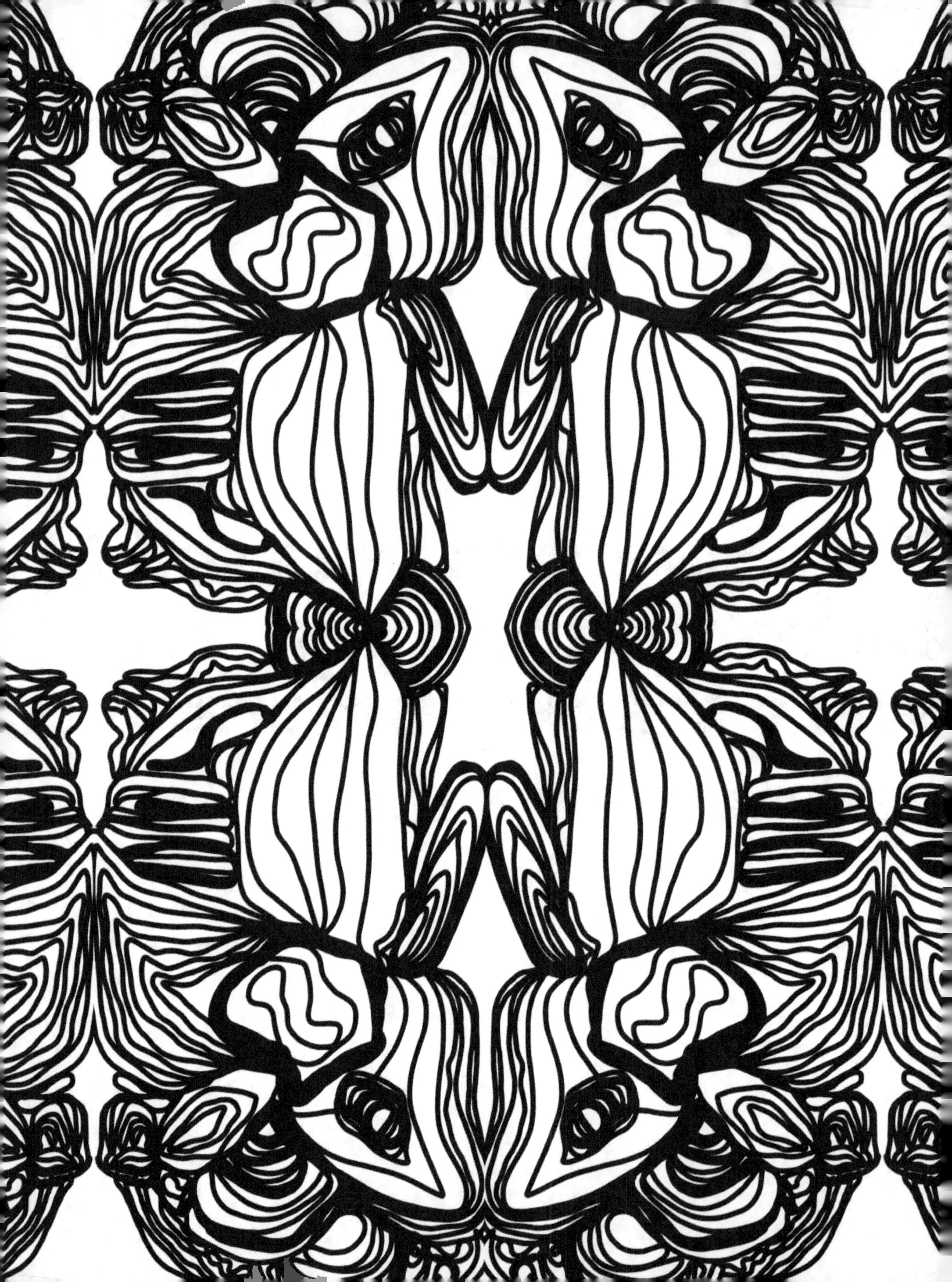

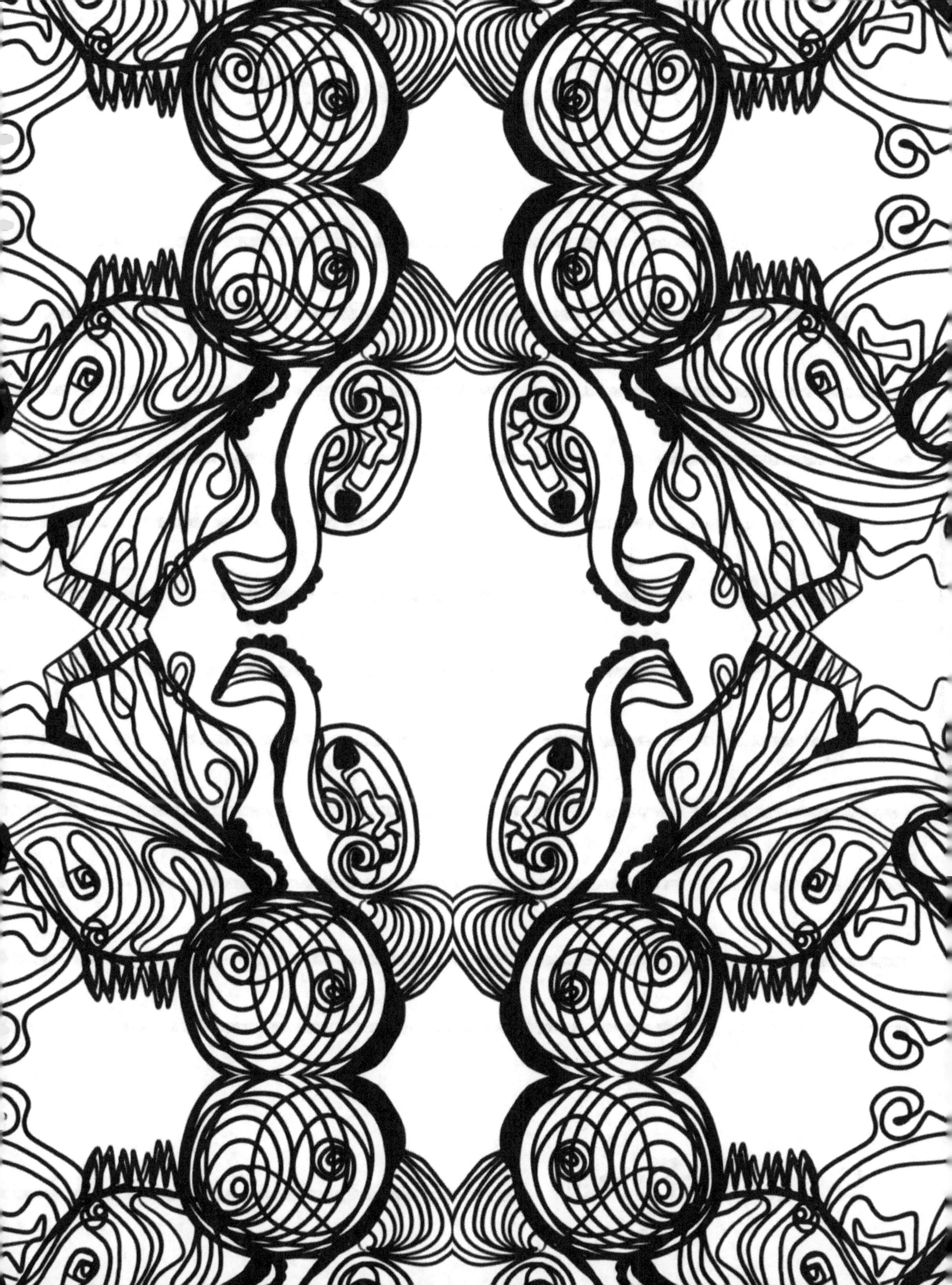

What do I believe about my future?

____

____

____

____

____

____

____

____

____

____

____

Date & Time _______________________

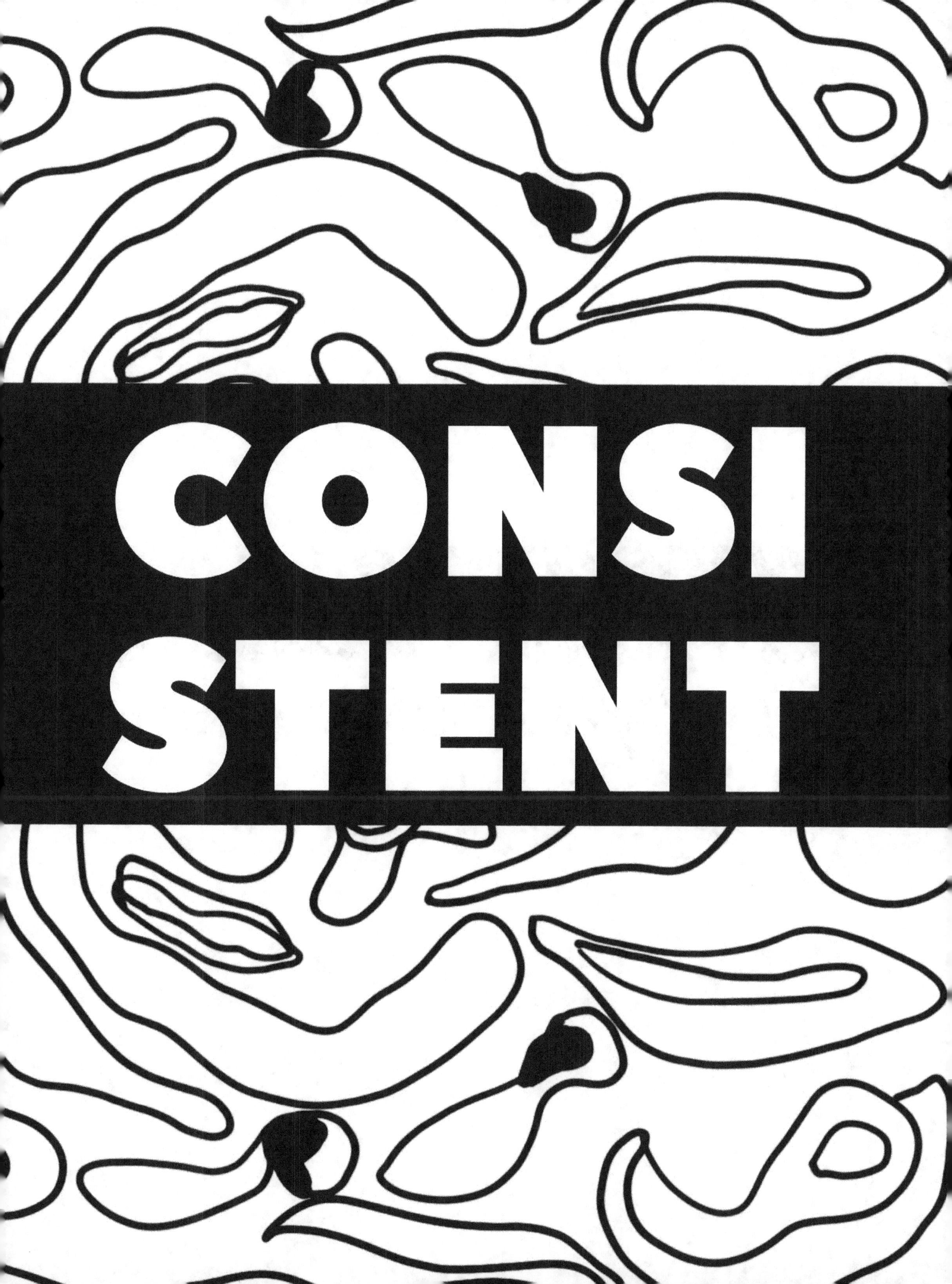
CONSI
STENT

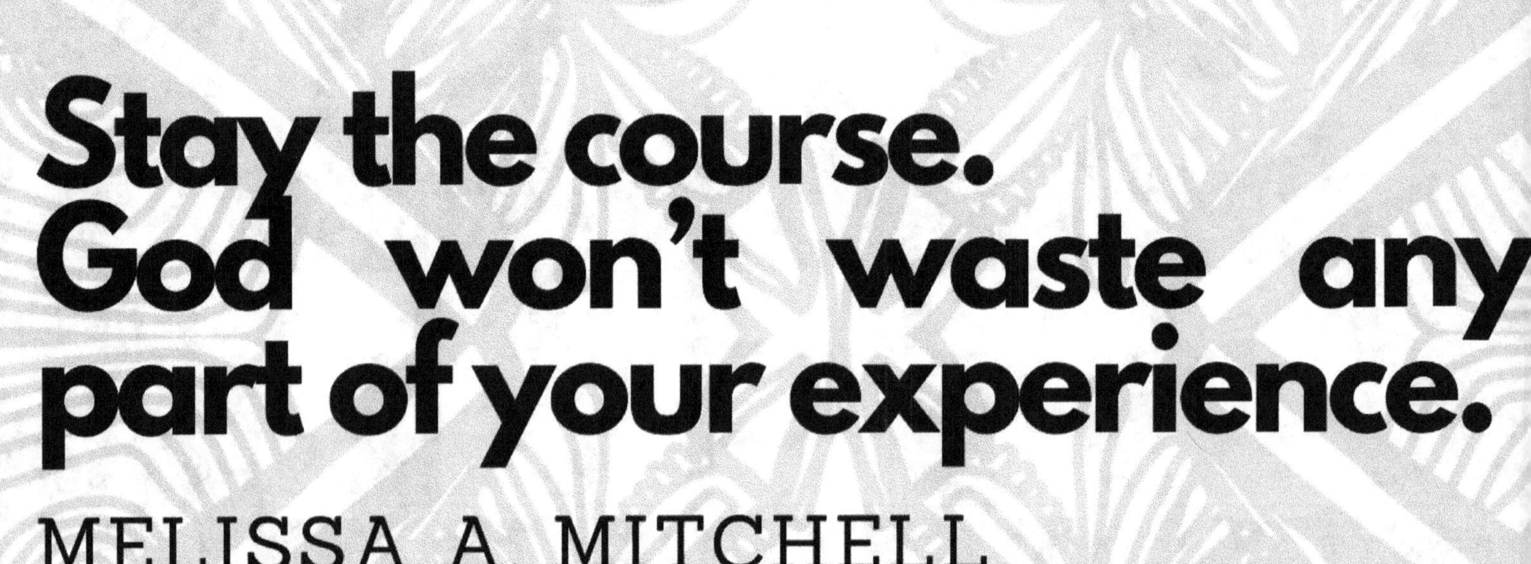

Stay the course. God won't waste any part of your experience.

MELISSA A. MITCHELL

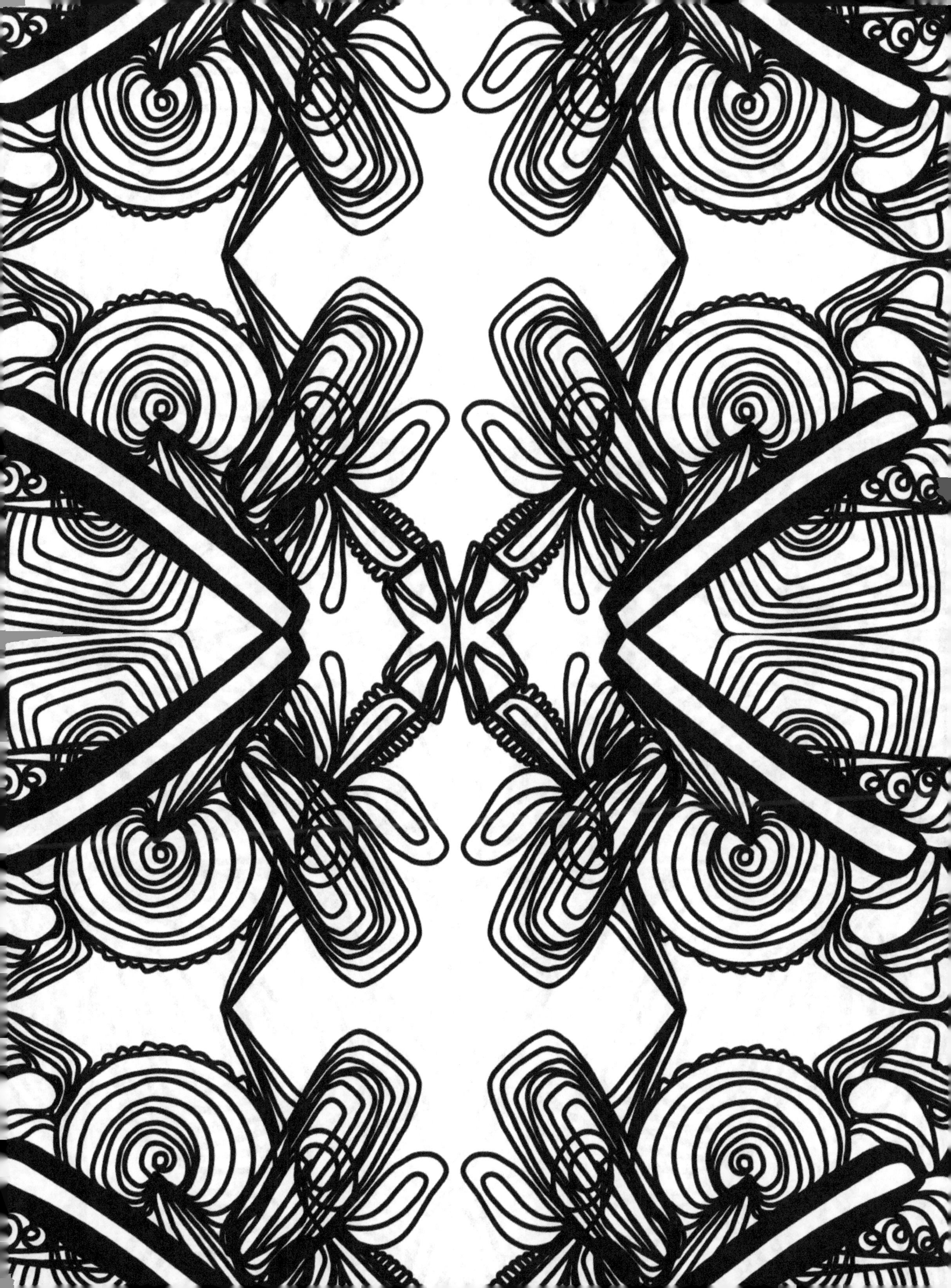

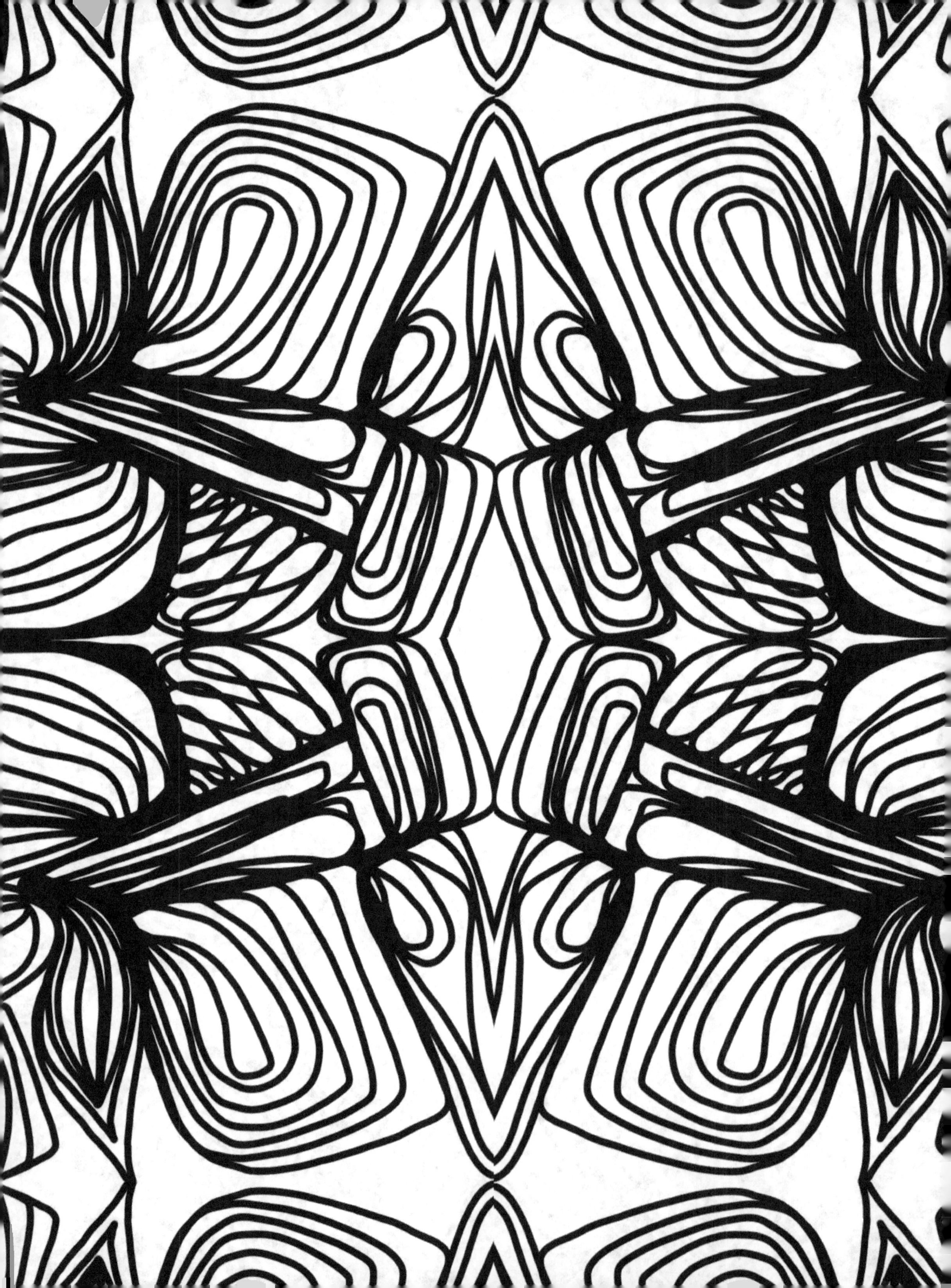

What must I consistently do to see my dreams come to life?

____

____

____

____

____

____

____

____

____

____

Date & Time _______________________

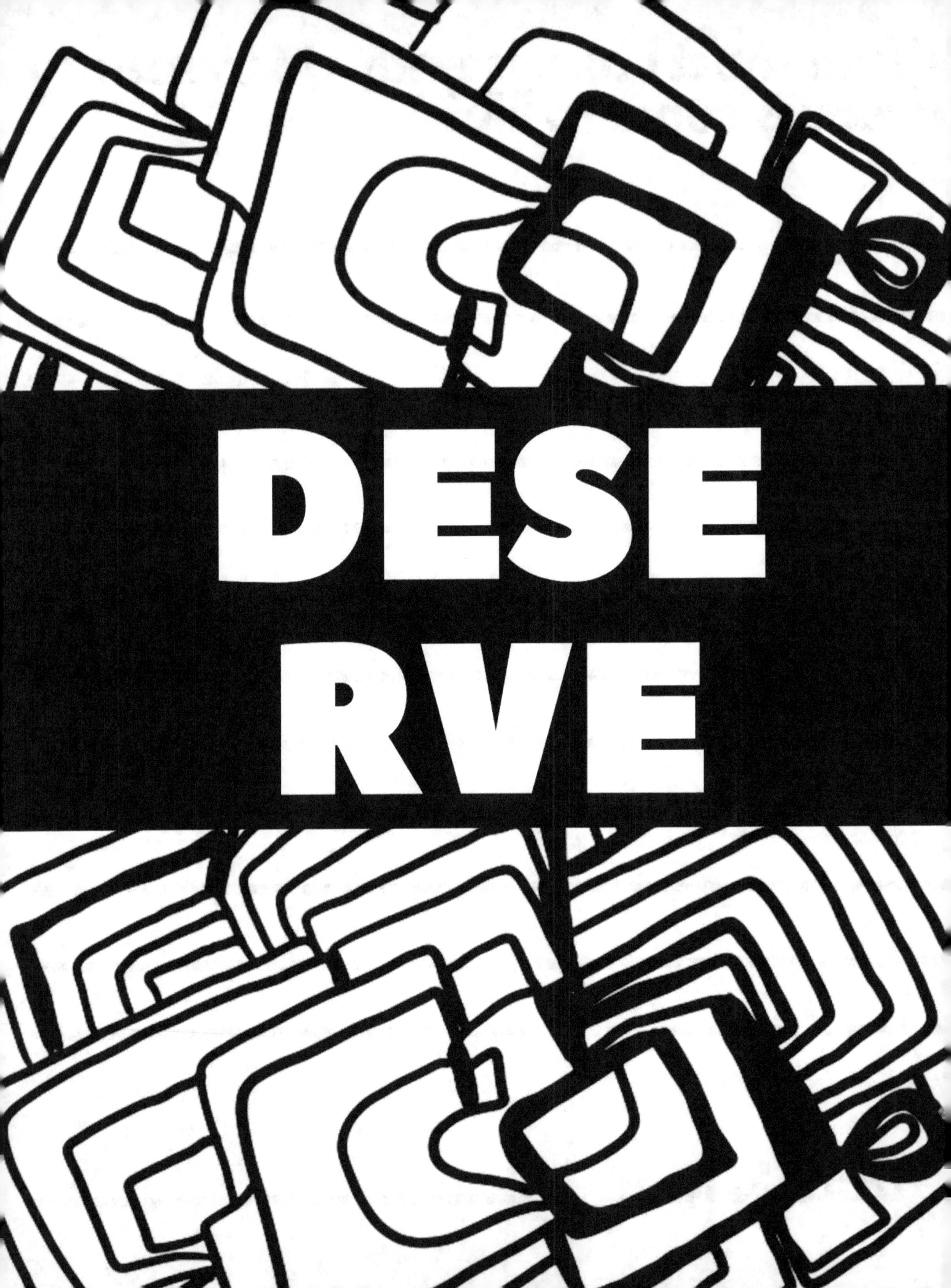
DESE
RVE

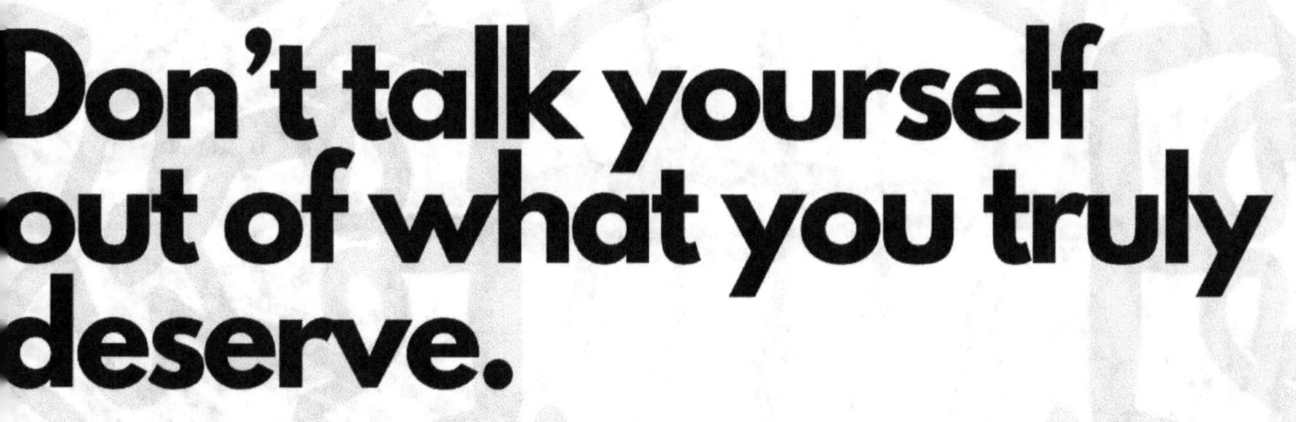

MELISSA A. MITCHELL

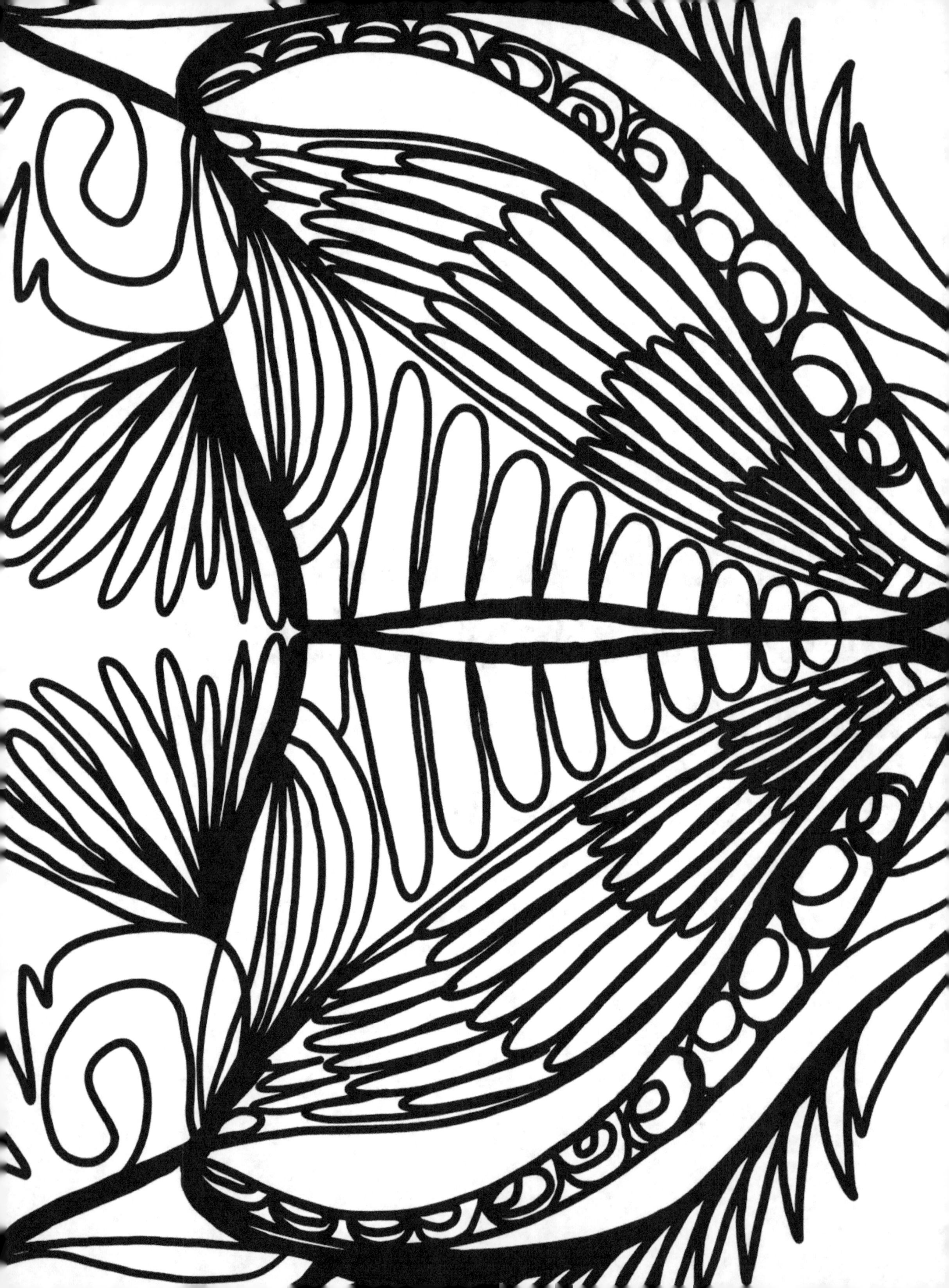

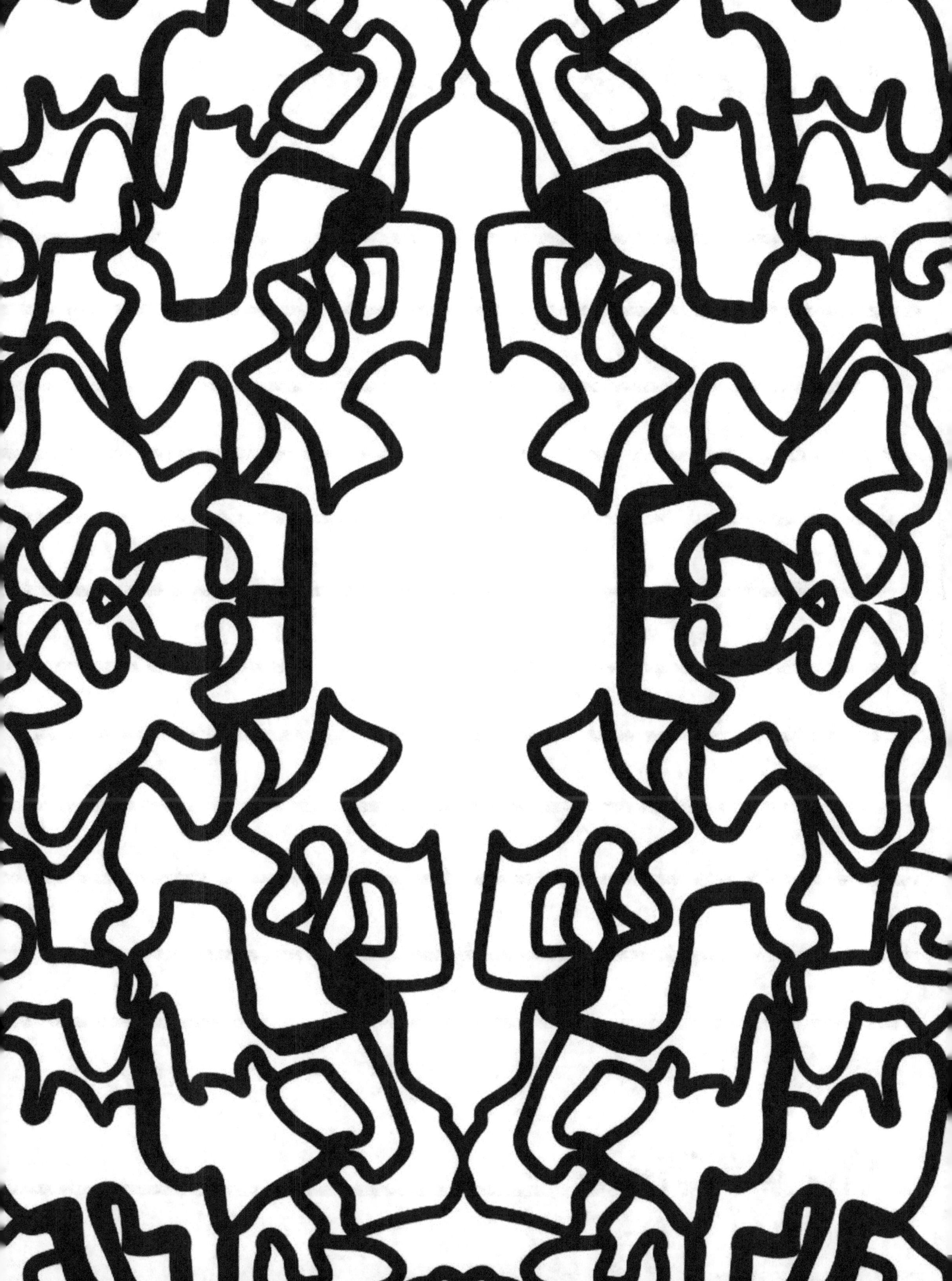

What am I most deserving of?

Date & Time _______________

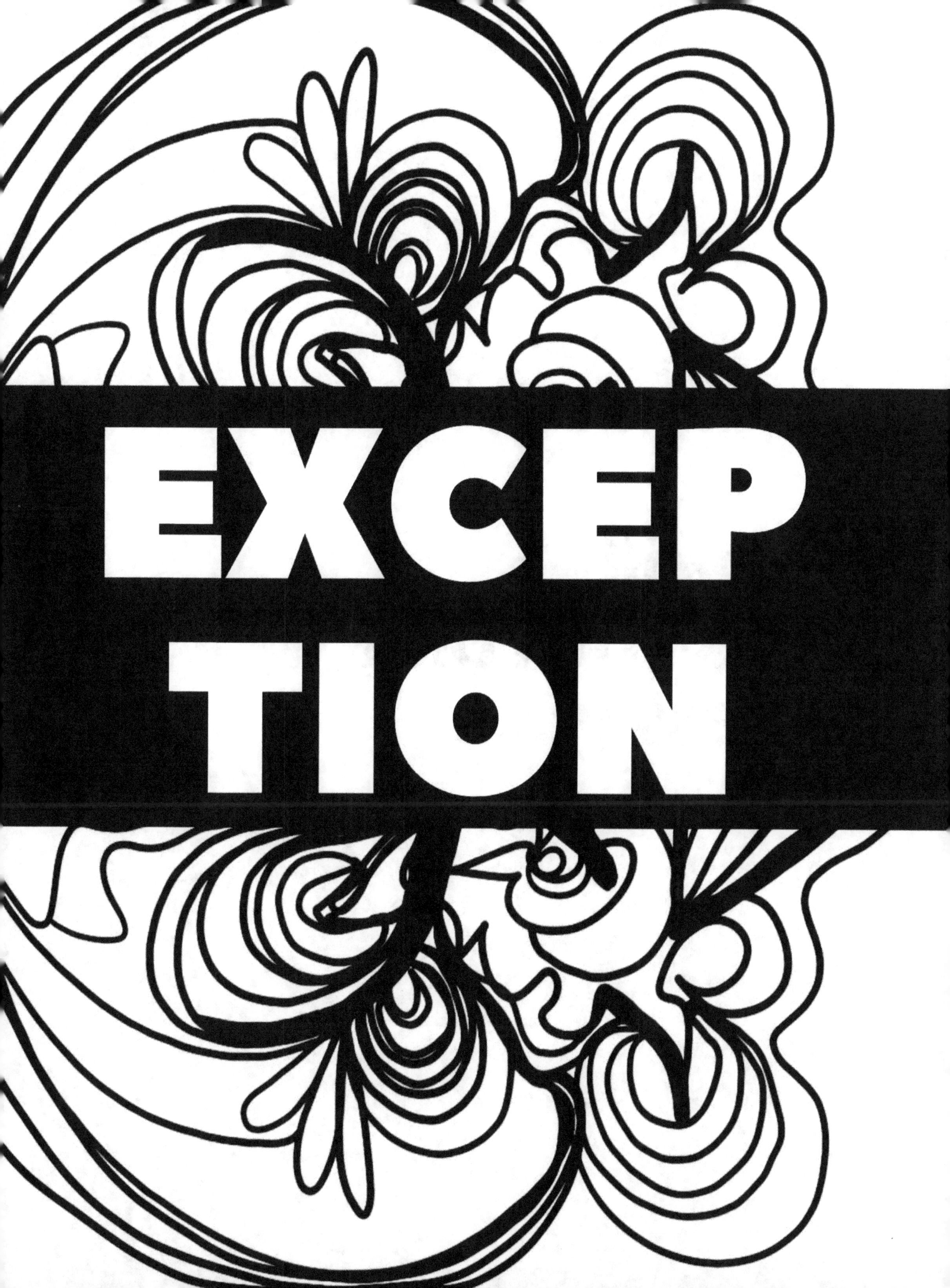
EXCEP
TION

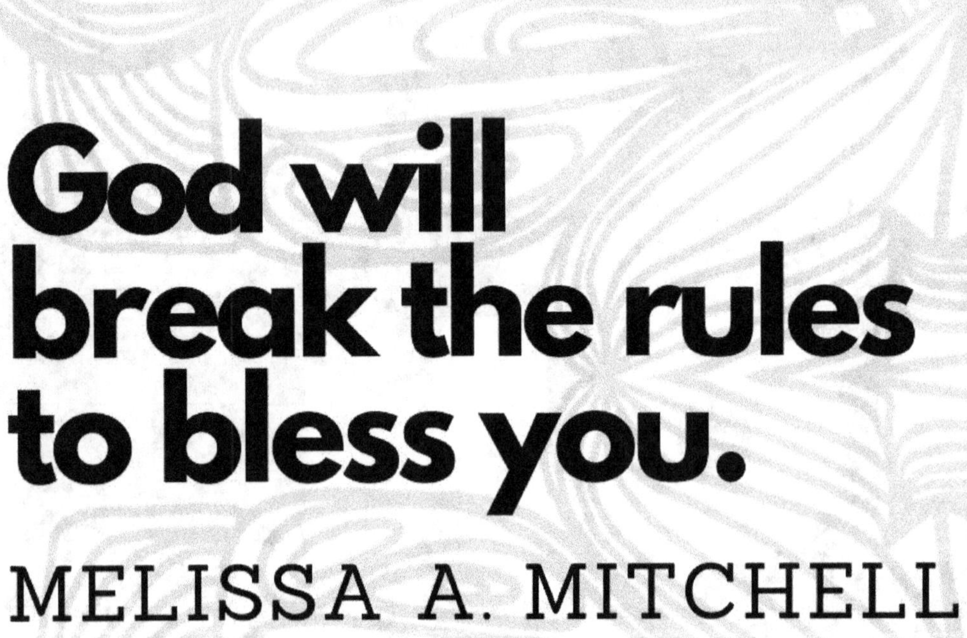

God will break the rules to bless you.

MELISSA A. MITCHELL

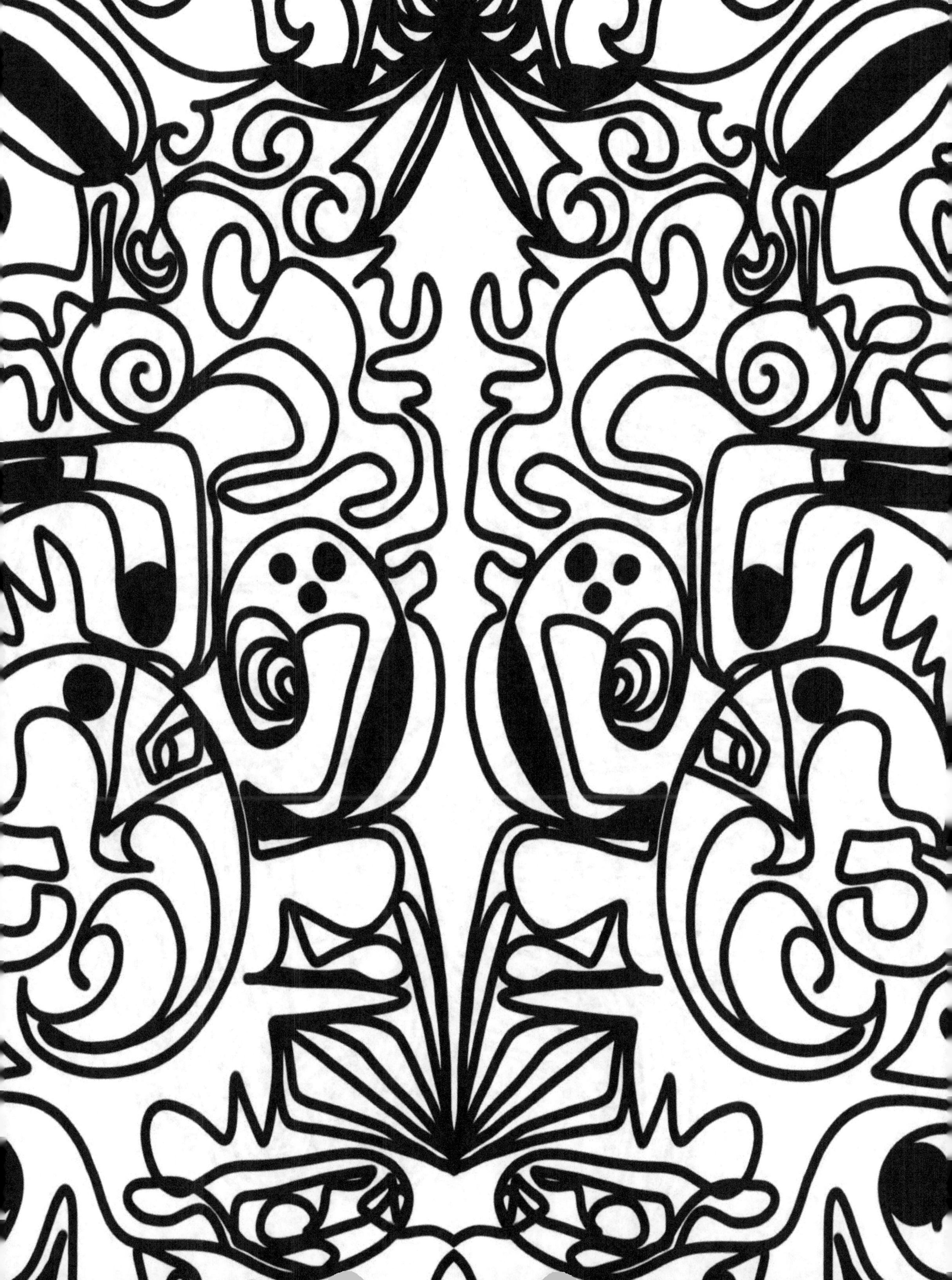

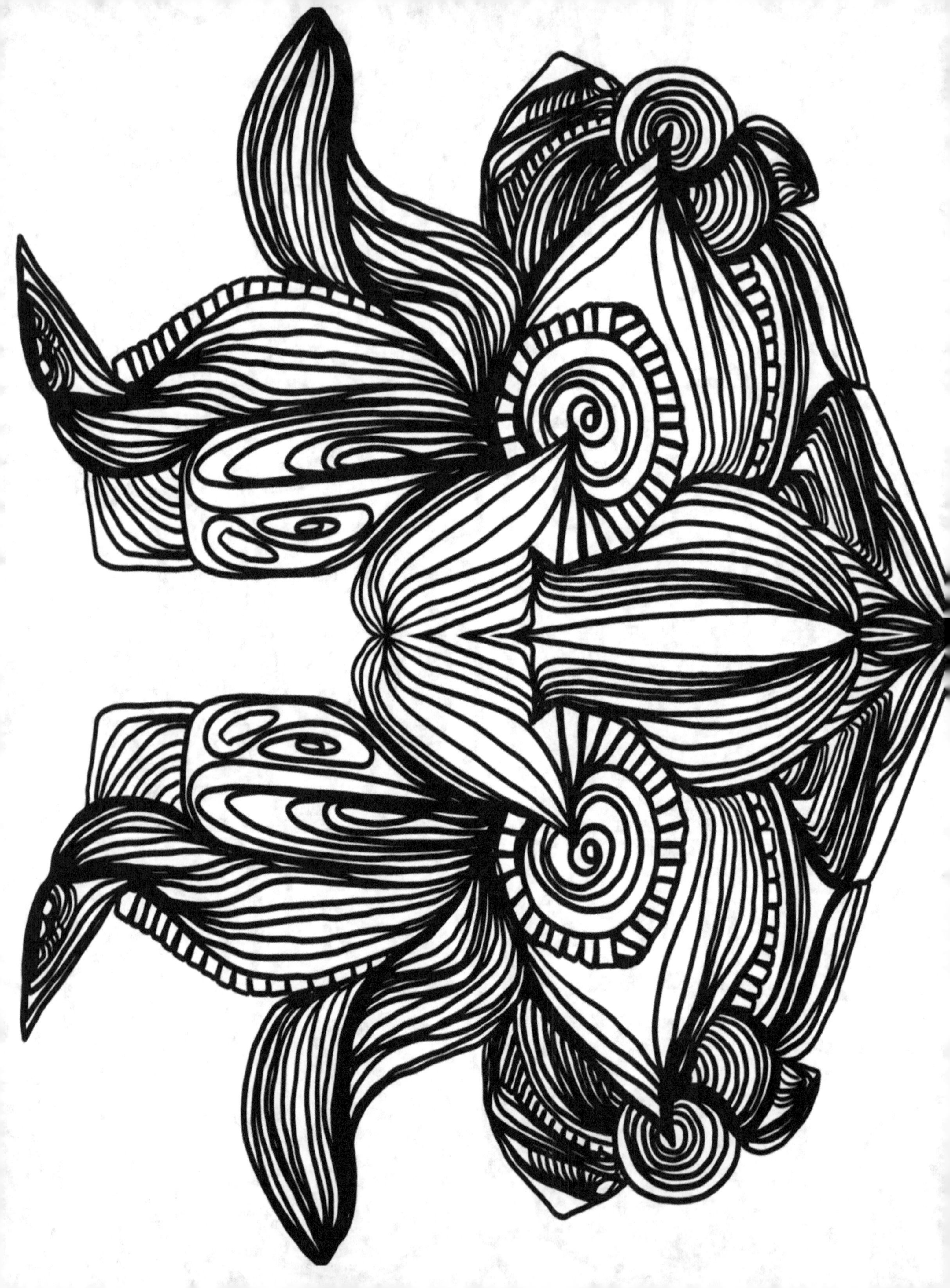

How will my life's story inspire others?

Date & Time ___

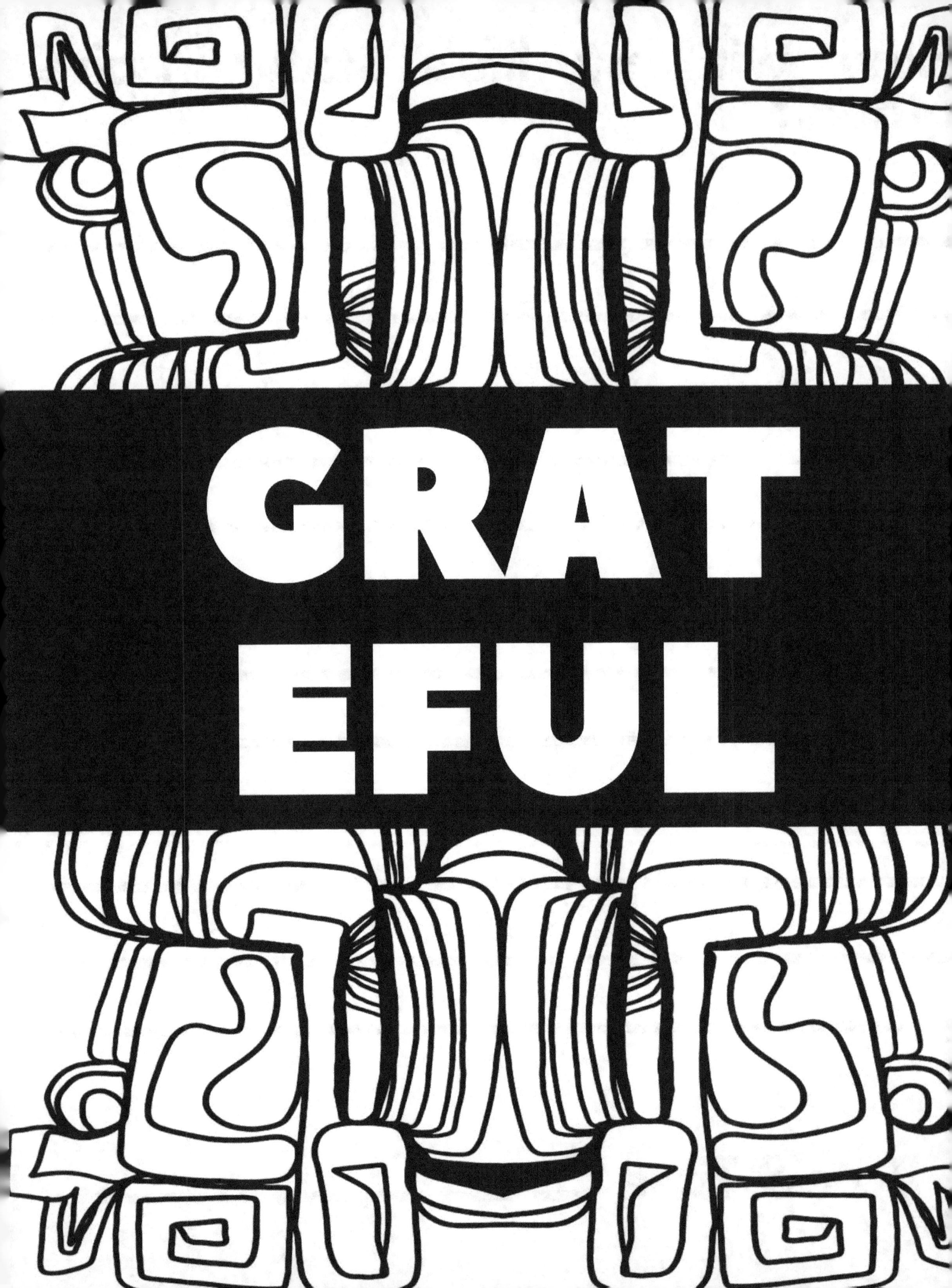
GRAT
EFUL

Be grateful for even the smallest things, and watch them grow into bigger things to be grateful for.

MELISSA A. MITCHELL

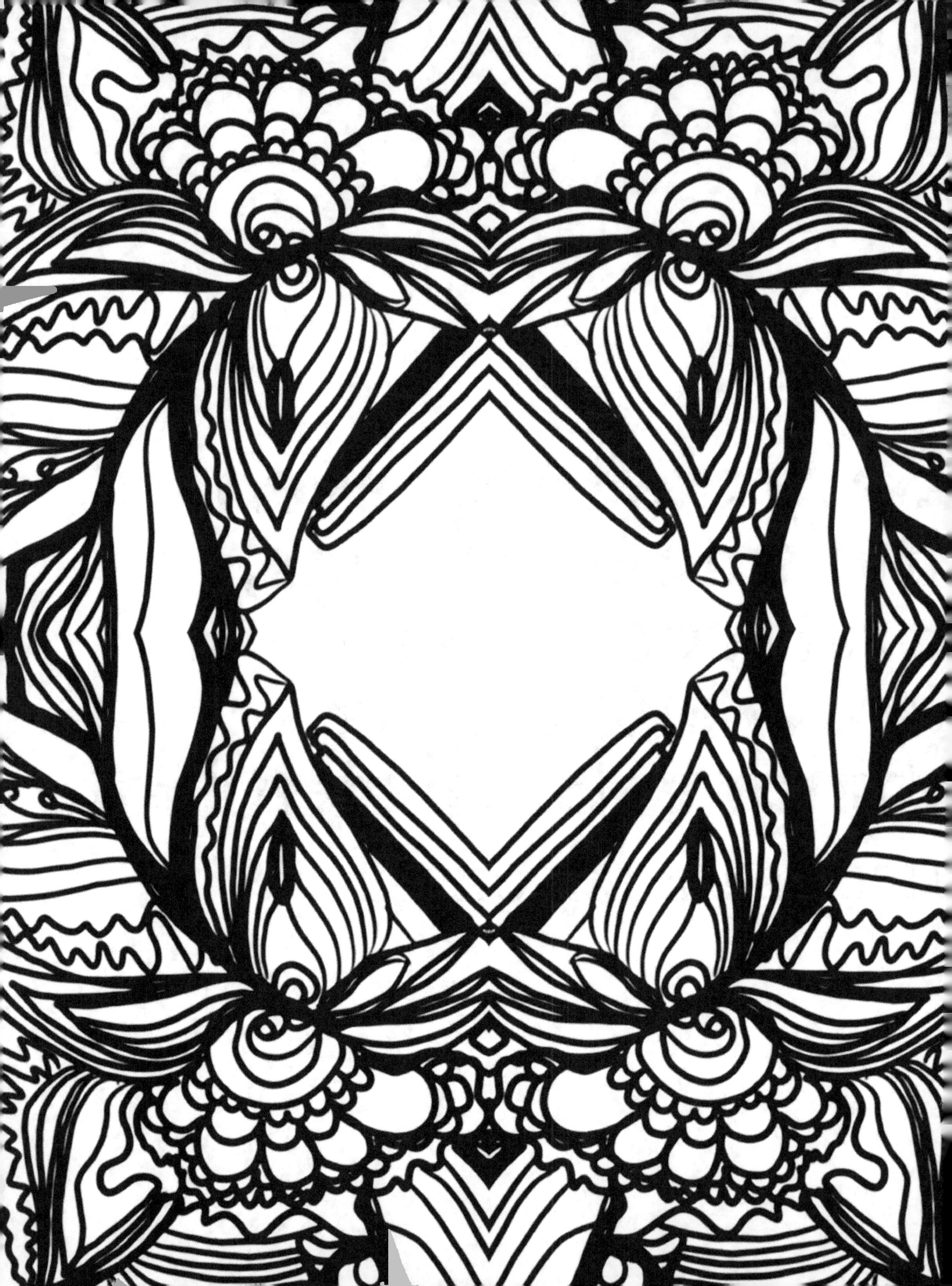

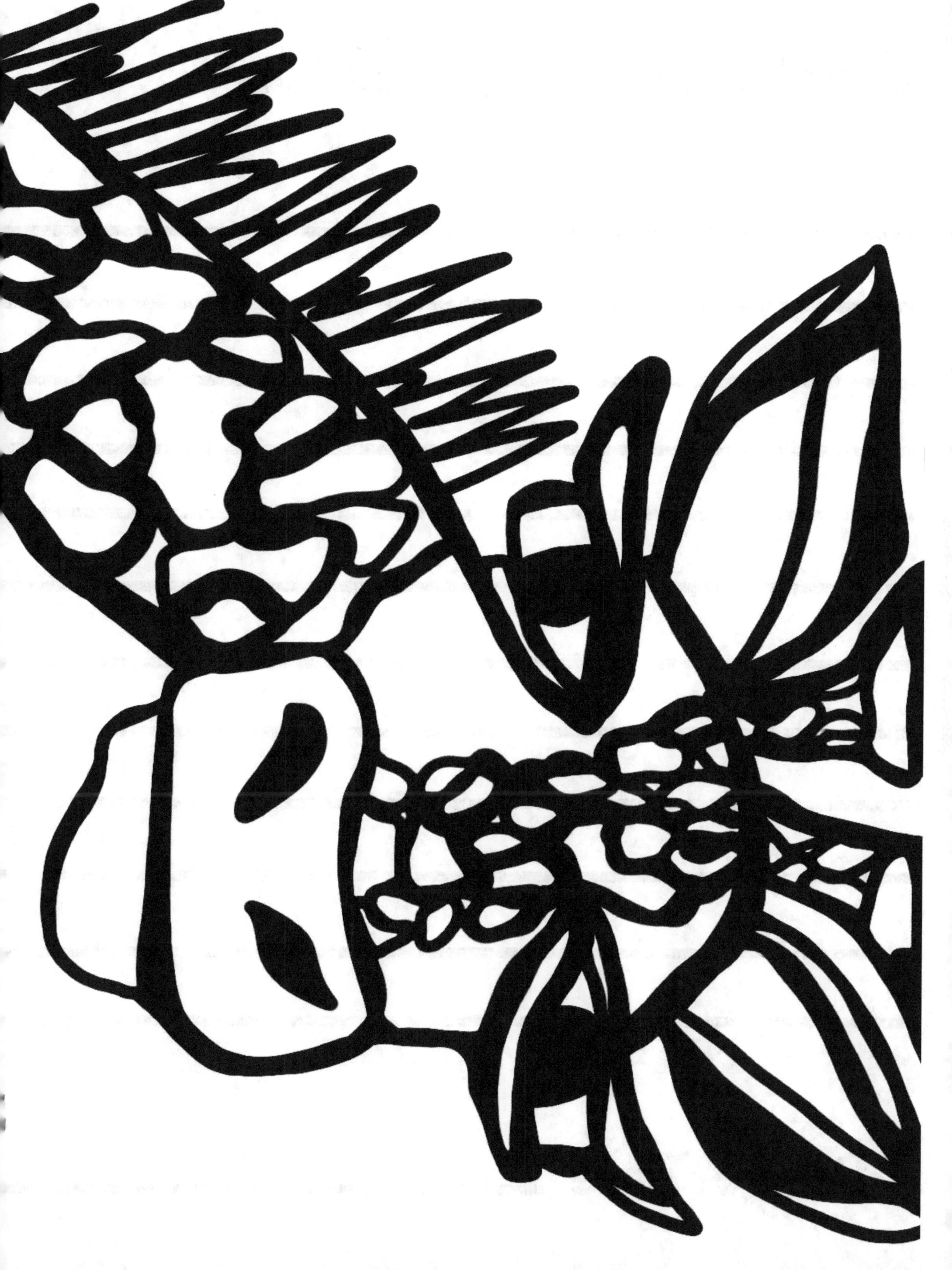

What am I most grateful for?

____

____

____

____

____

____

____

____

____

____

Date & Time _______________________

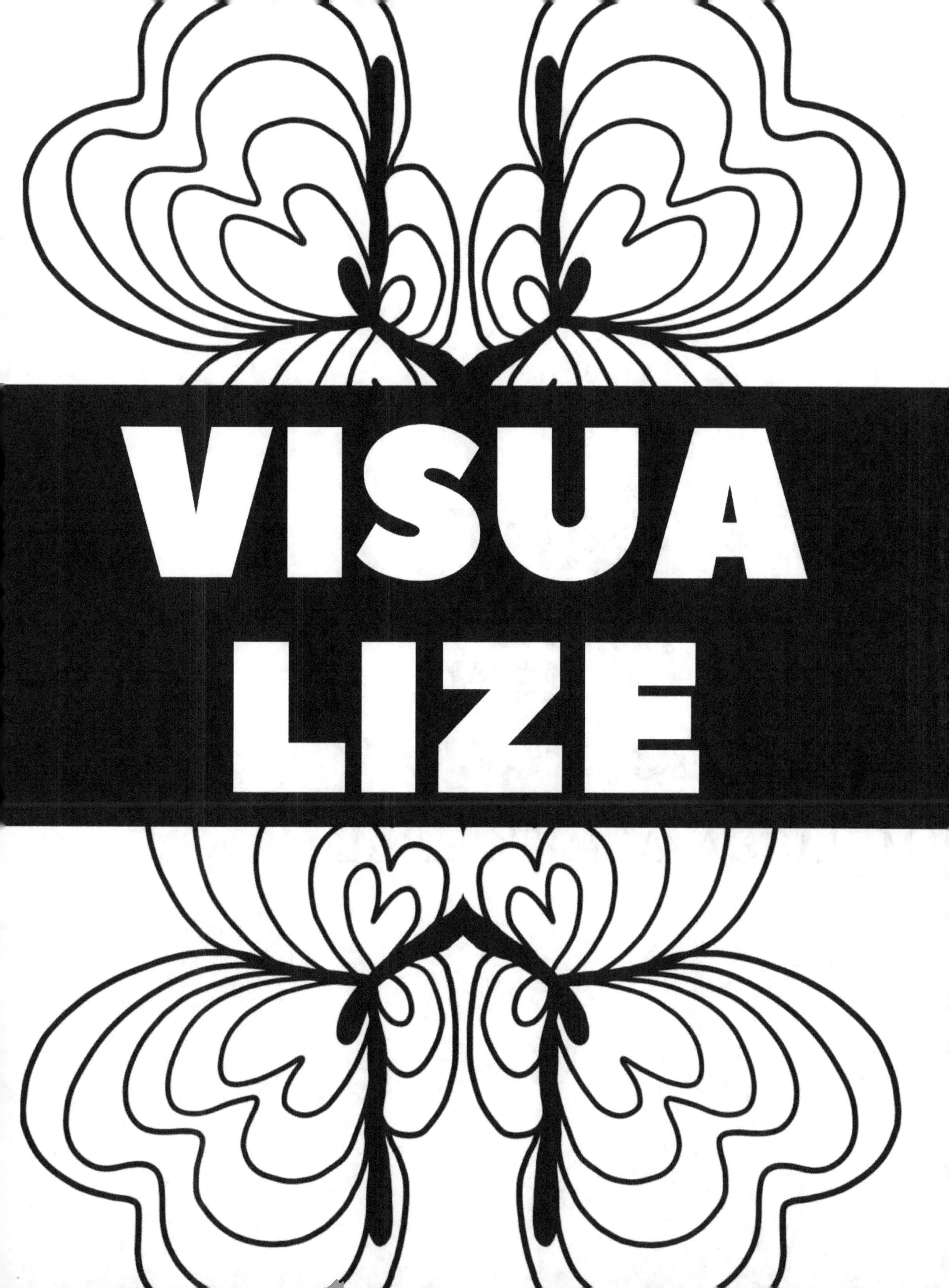

VISUA
LIZE

Think bigger, dream bigger, speak bigger, become bigger.

MELISSA A. MITCHELL

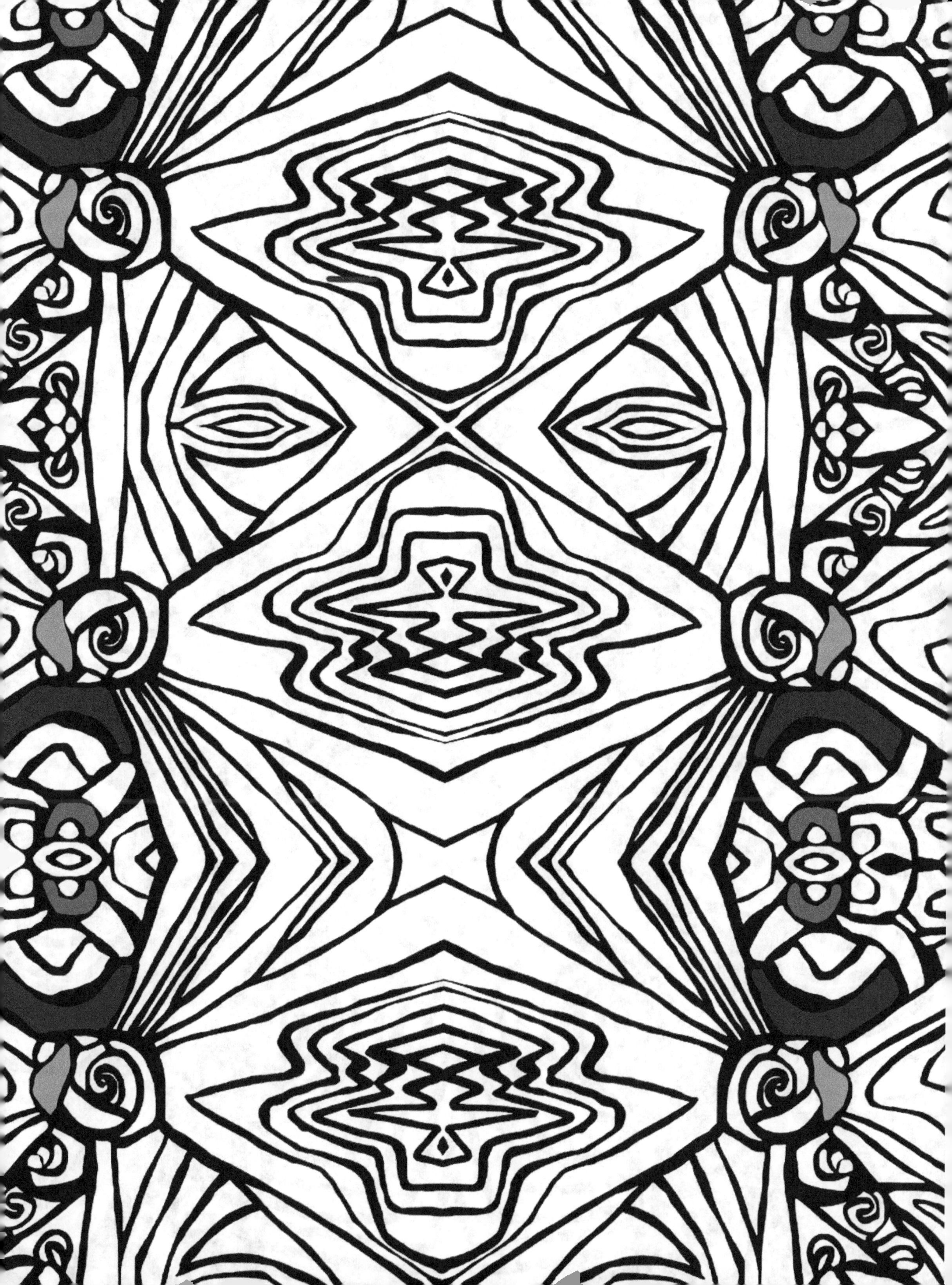

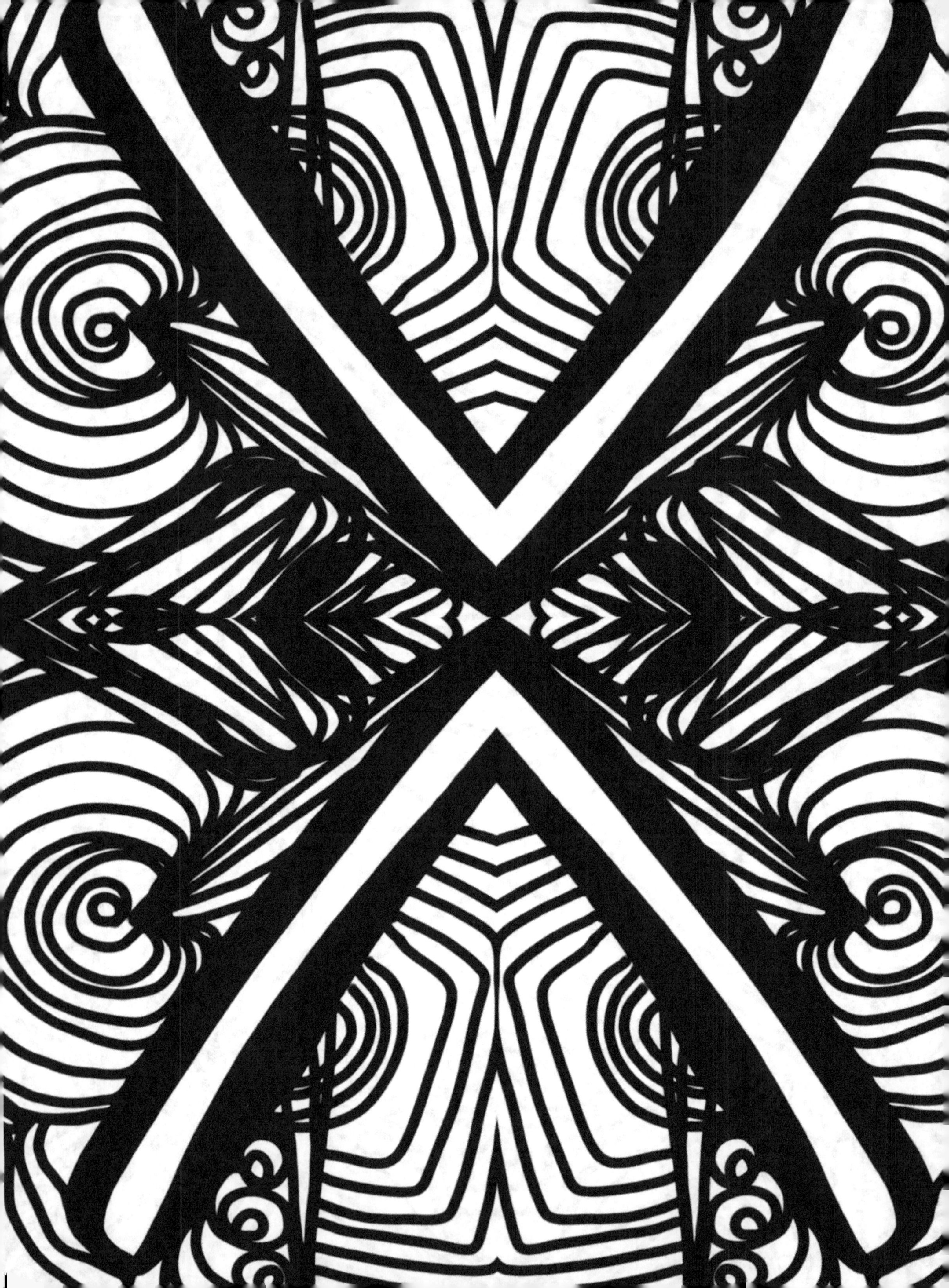

How do I visualize my future?

Date & Time _______________________

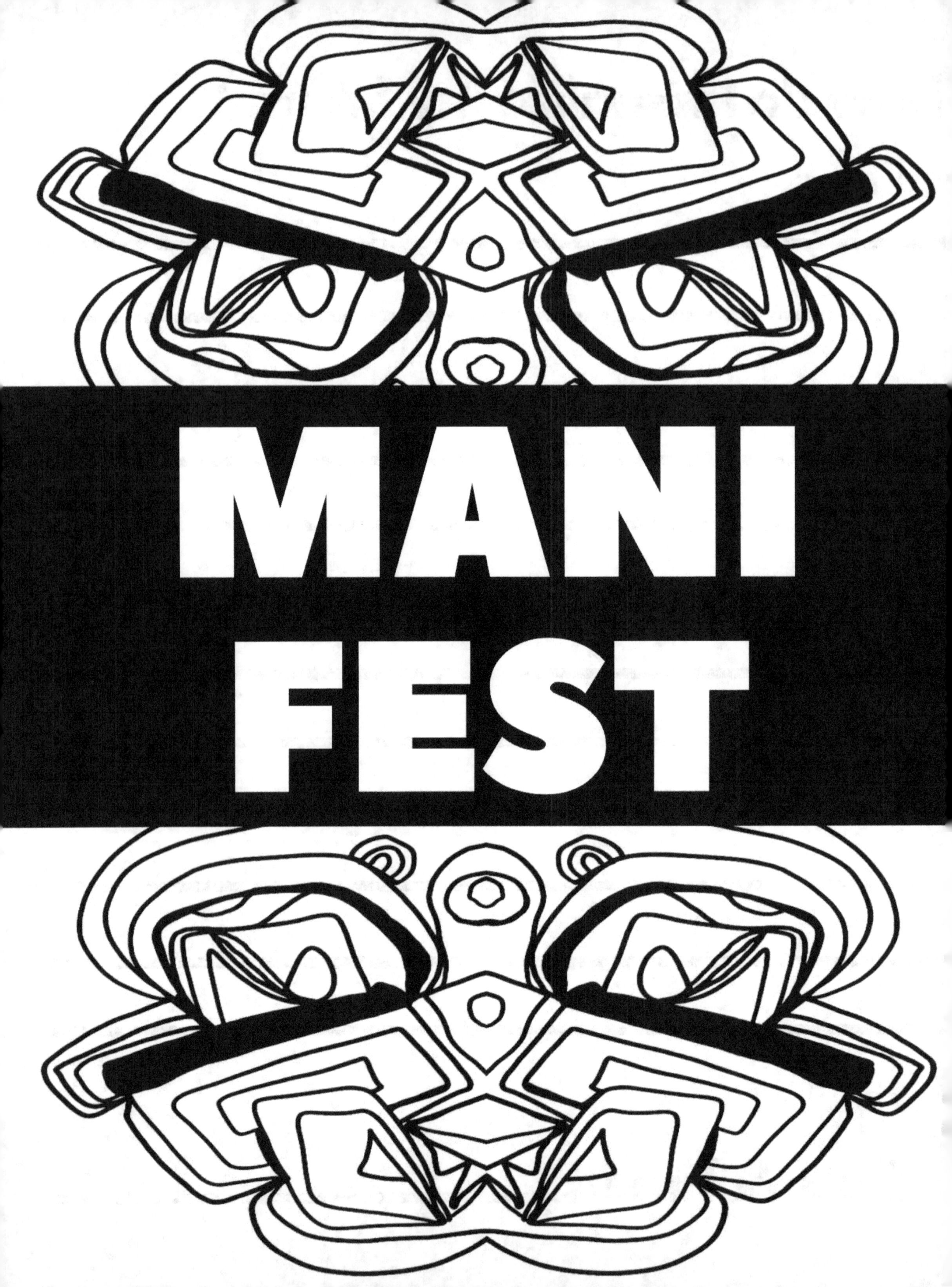

MANI
FEST

Nothing I ask for is beyond God's ability to manifest.

MELISSA A. MITCHELL

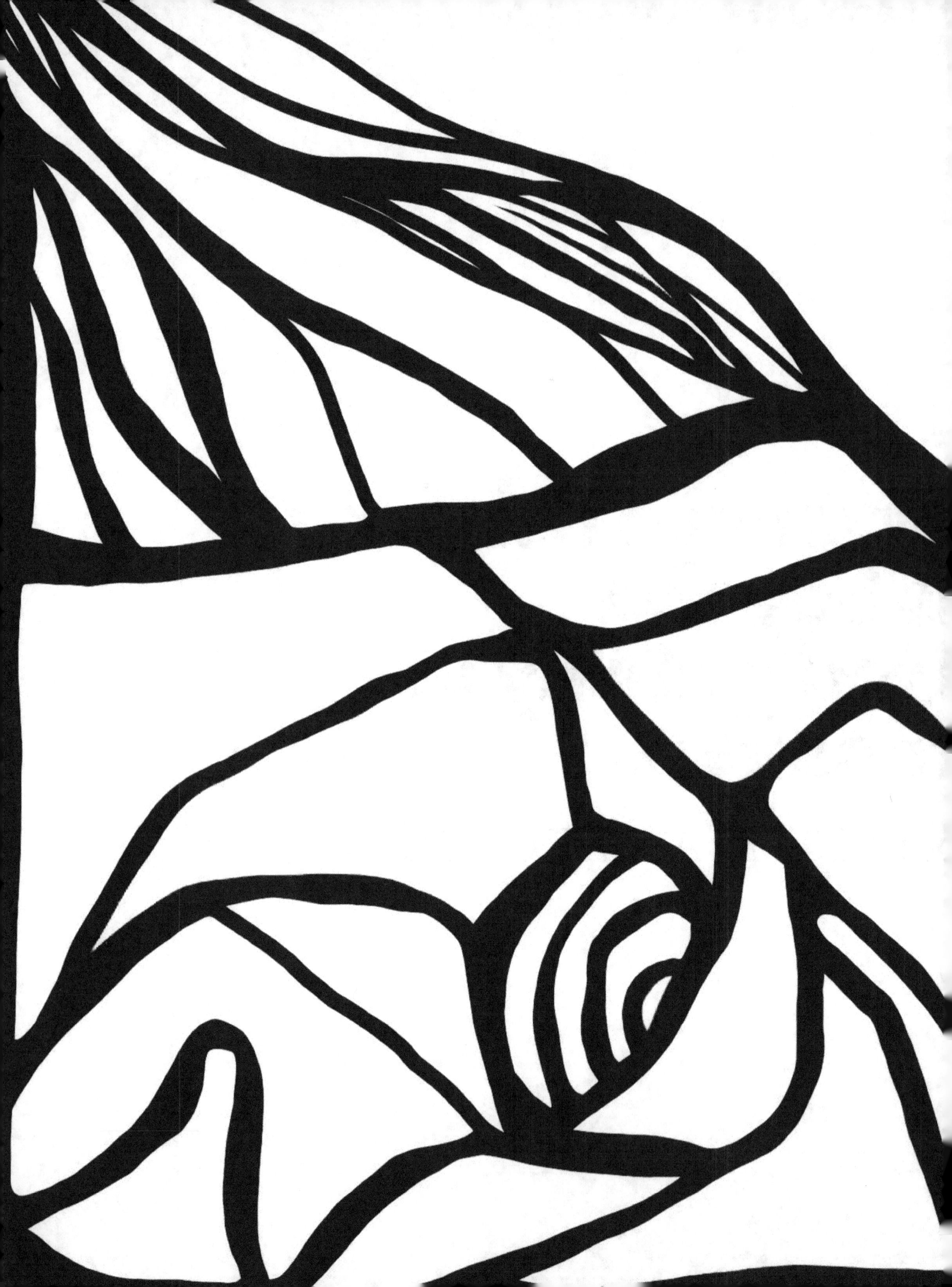

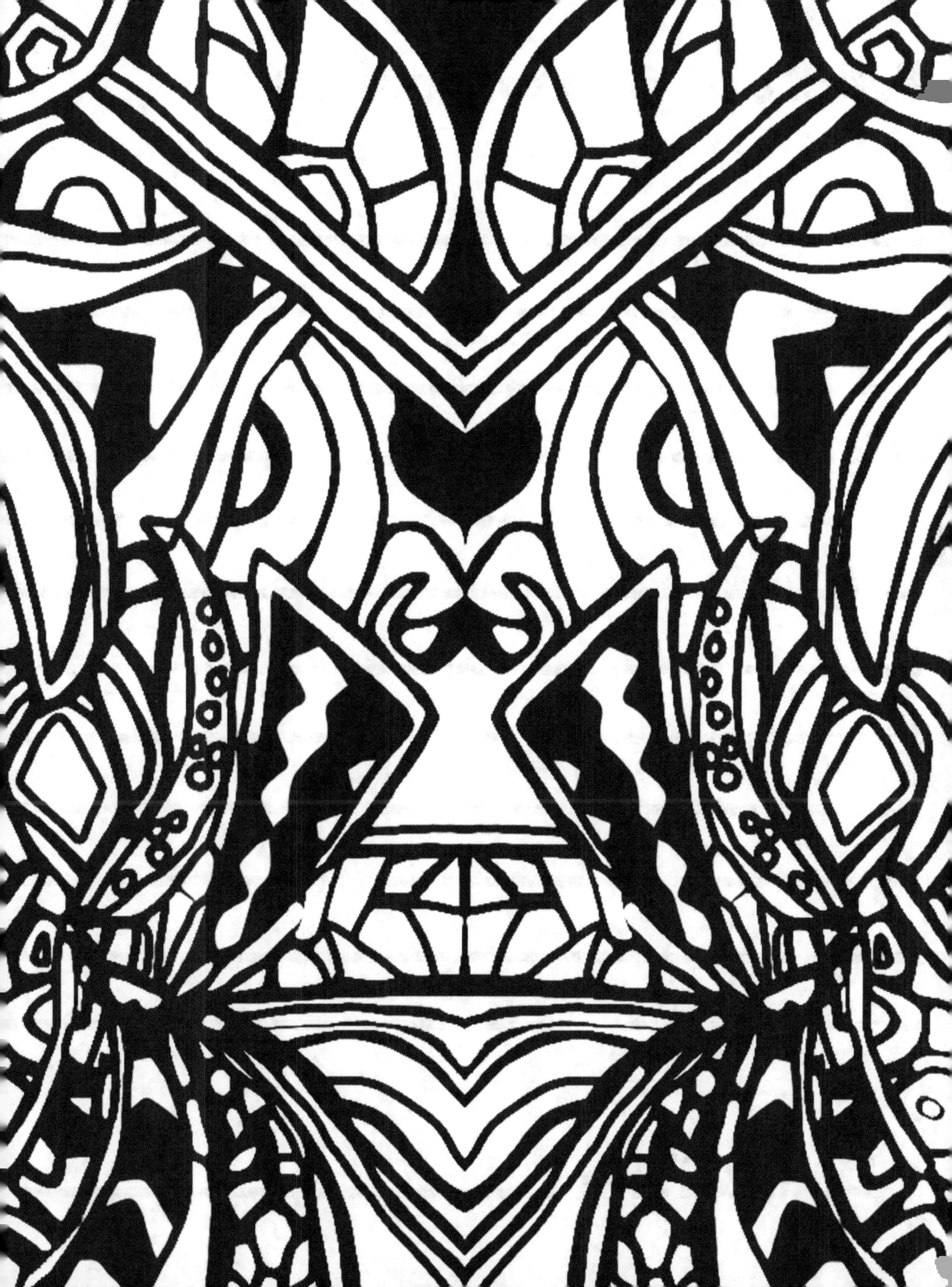

What do I plan to manifest?

Date & Time ________________

Nothing is more beautiful than manifesting your wildest dreams. If you stay the course, truly believe, and remain unwavering in your pursuit, God will blow your mind in ways beyond your expectation.

I hope Color and Manifest mentally catapults you to a new dimension of thinking, being, and believing. Continue to keep your goals in front of you every single day because there is inherent power in reading, writing, reciting—and even coloring—your dreams.

I pray you harness the power to take control of the brush, and paint yourself into something beautiful.

Always remember...you are God's greatest masterpiece.

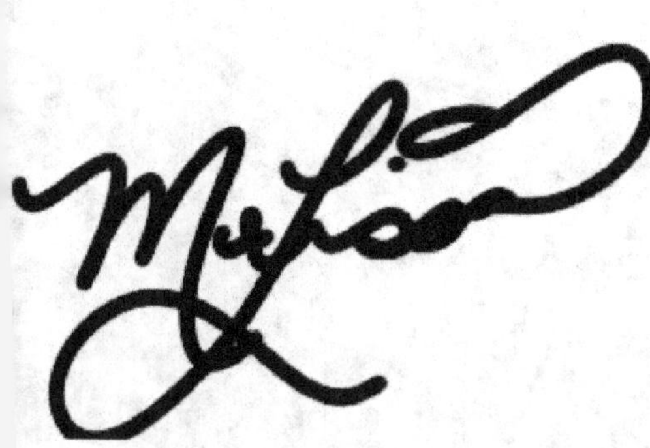

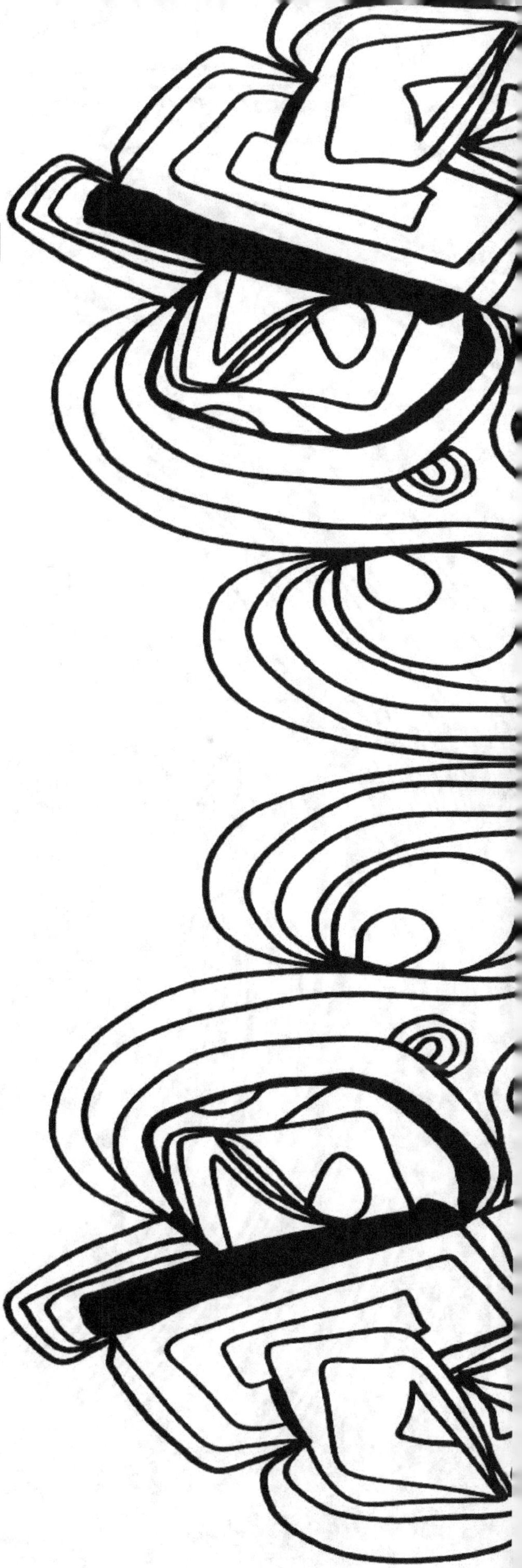

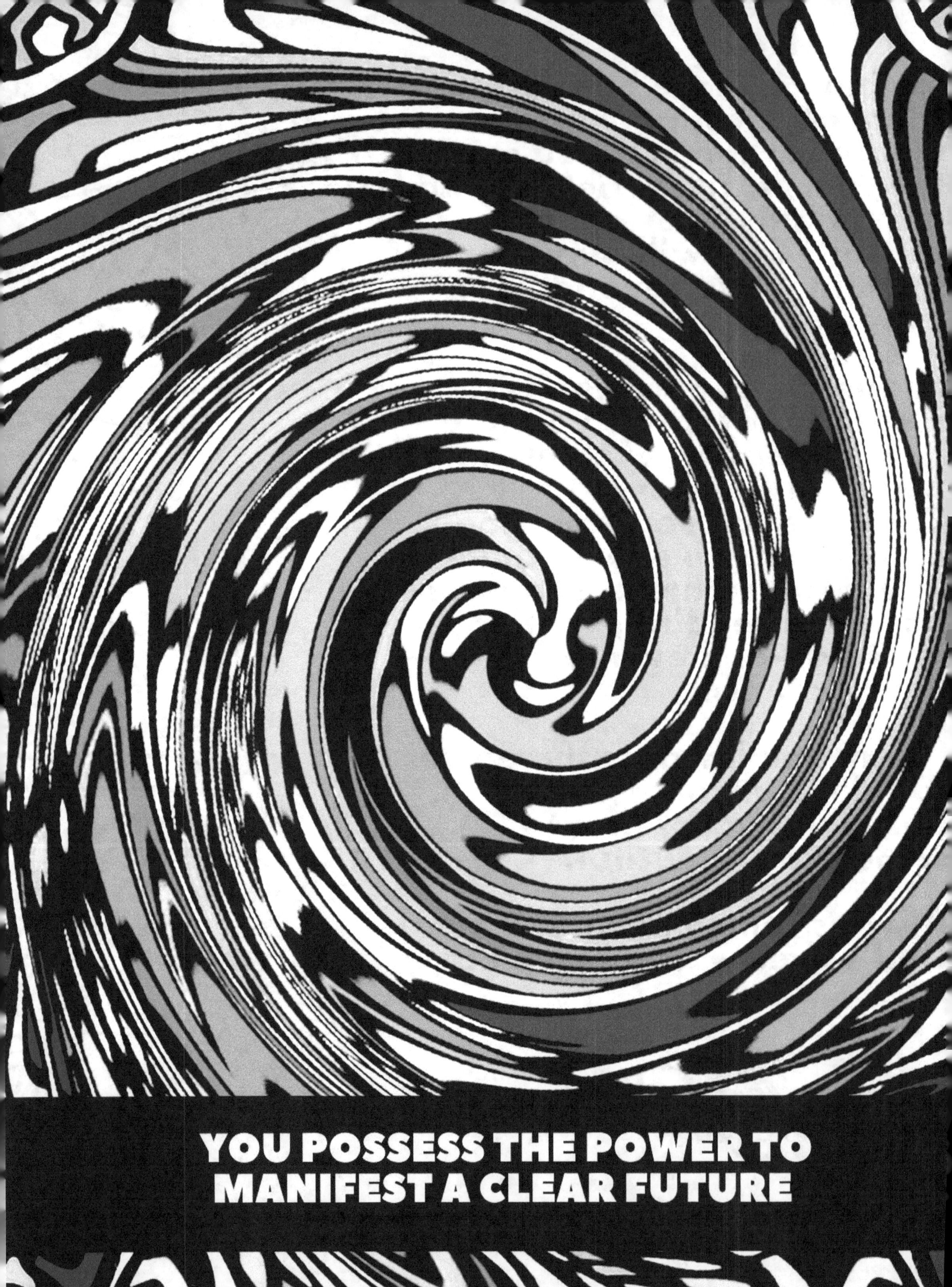
YOU POSSESS THE POWER TO MANIFEST A CLEAR FUTURE